Hare Kṛṣṇa Hare
Hare Rāma Hare

A Bouquet of Woeful Entreaties

Vilāpa Kusumāñjali

Śrī Śrīmad Bhaktivedānta
Nārāyaṇa Gosvāmī Mahārāja

Bhaktabandhav

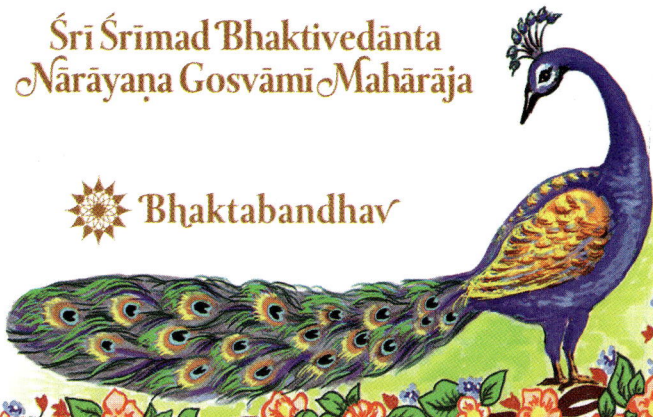

A BOUQUET OF WOEFUL ENTREATIES

Compiled from *hari-kathā* of Guru and Vaiṣṇavas by Das Anudas

First Edition printing: 1,000 copies, Gaura Purṇimā, 2013

Second Edition printing: 2,000 copies, Kātyayani-vrata 2015

Printing sponsored by Śrīman Jagannātha dāsa Punja (Fiji), in memory of his good wife, Kṛṣṇa-līlā devī dāsī.

In 1974, Śrīman Jagannātha Punja and Śrīmati Kṛṣṇa-līlā devī dāsī of Fiji first came to Vṛndāvana and there obtained Deities of Rādhā-Kṛṣṇa and began worshipping Them. In 1975, Śrīīa Bhaktivedānta Svāmī Prabhupāda went to their house in Fiji. They served Prabhupāda and he was very pleased with them. Again in 1976 Prabhupāda went to their house and gave them harināma. They had a strong desire to take dīkṣā from Śrīla Prabhupāda, however, before they were able to, Śrīla Prabhupāda entered samādhi. In 1997, twenty years later, Śrī Śrīmad Bhaktivedānta Nārāyaṇa Gosvāmī Mahārāja Śrīla Gurudeva came to their home in Fiji. Meeting with him, they experienced that he was non-different from Śrīla Svāmī Prabhupāda. They asked for dīkṣā from Śrīla Gurudeva. He said to them, "Those who have once met with Svāmī Prabhupāda I consider his disciples." "Yes, this is true," they responded, "but we accept you as our Gurudeva." They served Śrīla Gurudeva so much and he was extremely pleased with them. In 2010, on October 6th, after taking darśana of Sevā-kuñja, Rādhā-Dāmodara, Imli-tala, and Rūpa-Sanātana Gauḍīya Maṭha, Śrī Kṛṣṇa-līlā Devī left her body in Gopinātha-bhavana. In this way, she entered kṛṣṇa-līlā to serve Śrīla Gurudeva there and prepare for his arrival.

www.bhaktabandhav.com

Śrī Kṛṣṇa Caitanya Prabhu Nityānanda Śrī Advaita Gadādhara Śrīvāsadi Gaura-bhakta-vṛnda
Hare Kṛṣṇa Hare Kṛṣṇa Kṛṣṇa Kṛṣṇa Hare Hare Hare Rāma Hare Rāma Rāma Rāma Hare Hare

Śrīla Raghunātha dāsa Gosvāmī's
Vilāpa-kusumāñjali

A Bouquet of Woeful Entreaties

A Bhāva-anukula-smarana commentary

Manifested through the causeless mercy of he who is the best amongst the 11th generation in the *bhāgavata-paramparā* descending from Śrī Kṛṣṇa-Caitanya Mahāprabhu and who is the foremost bestower of *vraja-bhakti* in the modern age:

nitya-līlā-praviṣṭa-om-viṣṇupada paramārādhyatama rūpānuga-ācārya-varya bhakta-bāndhava

Śrī Śrīmad
Bhaktivedānta Nārāyaṇa Gosvāmī Mahārāja
by his disciples

nārāyaṇam gurum-vande śaranyam bhakta-bāndhavam
gaura-manobhiṣṭam pūrnam rādhā-dasyam-pradāyakam

I offer prayers unto Śrīla Gurudeva, Bhaktivedānta Nārāyaṇa Gosvāmī Mahārāja, who, as Bhakta-bāndhava, is the most worthy shelter for everyone. He fulfills the inner-heart desire of Gaurahari and bestows *rādhā-dasyam*, the position of being Rādhārāṇī's intimate maidservant.

gaurahari paraṁ-preṣṭha nityānanda abhinnaka
śrī-gaura-nārāyaṇa bhakta-bāndhava priya-sevaka

Śrī Gaura Nārāyaṇa is very dear to Śrī Gaurahari and is a non-different manifestation of Nityānanda Prabhu. He is the friend of all devotees and the dearest of *sevakas*.

sevā kuñje vraje ramye govardhana girau sadā
rādhā kuṇḍe rasānande tat tat sevā pradāyakam

Śrīla Gurudeva is eternally residing in the beautiful Sevā-kuñja of Vraja, at Giri Govardhana, and at Rādhā-kuṇḍa. There, he is immersed in the bliss of nectarean mellows or *rasa*, and he grants entrance into the service of Rādhā-Kṛṣṇa as Their maidservant.

guruṁ nārāyanākhyam tam vande vinoda preṣṭhakam
yat pāda smṛti mātrena dāmodara prasīdati

I pray to Śrīla Gurudeva, Bhaktivedānta Nārāyaṇa Gosvāmī Mahārāja, who is very dear to Śrī Vinoda Mañjari. Simply by remembering his lotus feet one pleases Śrī Śrī Rādhā-Dāmodara.

Śrī Śrīmad Bhaktivedānta Nārāyaṇa Gosvāmī Mahārāja

namo sajjana sevaka sajjana preṣṭhāya bhūtale
śrī śrīmad bhaktivedānta vāmana iti nāmine

I offer my *pranāmas* unto Śrī Śrīmad Bhaktivedānta Vāmana Gosvāmī Maharāja, who is also known as Śrī Sajjan Sevaka, a dear servant to all saintly people of this world.

guru-dhāmni ca sevāsu vaiṣṇave sarvadā mati
granthe-bhāgavate-sākṣāt gosvāmī-vedānte-rati

Śrīla Vāmana Gosvāmī Mahārāja eternally serves the holy *dhāma* and Śrī Gurudeva, and his mind is always absorbed in serving the Vaiṣṇavas. He is the embodiment of the *Bhāgavatam*, the Vedic Scriptures, and the literature of the Gosvāmīs, and he possesses deep *rati* for them.

śac-cidānandamaya guruṁ mādhavāśraya vigraha
sambandhābhideya prayo-jana patha pradarśaka

He is *śac-cidānandamaya* (the guardian and preacher of the Bhaktivinoda-dhara). By his love he protects and nourishes those who have taken shelter of Śrī Śrī Rādhā-Mādhava, and he reveals the path of *sambandha*, *abhidheya*, and *prayojana*.

gaura-bhāvamaya tanu ujjvalarasa bhāvaka
bhaktivedānta vāmano rāga-bhakti-pravartaka

Śrīla Bhaktivedānta Vāmana Gosvāmī Mahārāja is so absorbed in *gaura-bhāva* that his complexion is the same as Śrī Gaurāṅga's; he is always immersed in *unnato-ujjvala-rasa*, and he distributes *anurāgamayi-bhakti*.

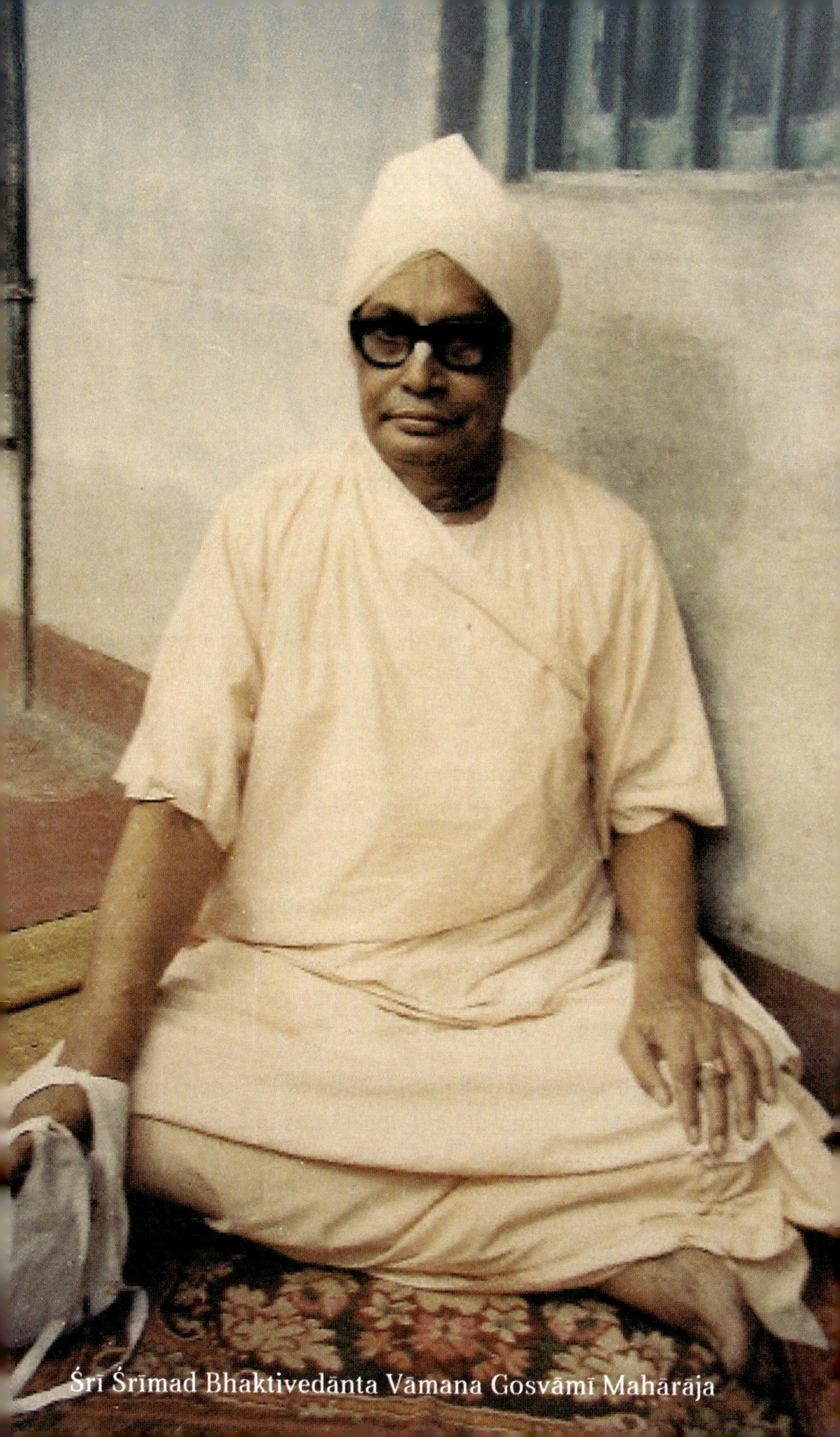

Śrī Śrīmad Bhaktivedānta Vāmana Gosvāmī Mahārāja

vajrād api kaṭhorāṇi go-govardhana-sevaka
mṛdūna kusumād api bhaktivedānta trivikrama

I offer my obeisances to Śrīla Bhaktivedānta Trivikrama Gosvāmī Mahārāja. Externally, he is grave and hard like Girirāja Govardhana, but his heart is softer than lotus petals. He is always engaged in *seva* and eternally serves the cows and Girirāja.

niṣkiñcana-jana-priya akiñcana suhṛda ca
ātmārāma-āptakāma avijñana muni sattama

Śrīla Trivikrama Gosvāmī Mahārāja has a sweet friendship with *niṣkiñcana* and *akiñcana* Vaiṣṇavas and they have so much affection for him. He is *atmārāma* and *aptakāma*, and is a learned scholar and *muni*. Always engaged in helping others, he gives pure knowledge and shows everyone how to follow the path of *bhakti*.

gaura-dhāma gaura-jana sevā-rata śrī trivikrama
nirantara anuśilana anugraha kṛpa-bhajana

Śrīla Trivikrama Gosvāmī Mahārāja continuously serves Gaura-dhāma and all of Śrīman Mahāprabhu's followers. He is a well-wisher of all souls and bestows transcendental blessings. By his mercy one can follow *bhakti*, but without receiving his mercy and following his example it is extremely difficult to enter the realm of pure *bhakti*.

guru-gaurāṅga-sadā-priya nityānanda-samārpita
māyāvādi-dharma-dhvaja smārta-pāṣaṇḍa pariśodaka

He is very dear to Guru-Gaurāṇga, and is surrended to the lotus feet of Nityānanda Prabhu. His merciful glance changes the conditioned nature of the *jīvas*. I offer him my unlimited *pranāmas*.

Śrī Śrīmad Bhaktivedānta Trivikrāma Gosvāmī Mahārāja

gāndharvike śrī rādhike
ahaṁ nityaṁ smarāmi
he gopike he vraja-devike
ahaṁ padaṁ anusmarāmi

I constantly meditate on Gāndharvikā Śrī Rādhikā and I follow the footsteps and always remember the lotus feet of the Vraja-devīs.

he hari-priye he vraja-vallabhe
hṛdayaṁ samarpayāmi
he kānu-priye he sakhī-priye
ahaṁ dāsyaṁ prārtayāmi

O Hari-priyā! O Vraja-vallabhā! I offer You my heart!
O Kānu-priya! O Sakhī-priyā! I pray for Your service!

he rādheśa he vrajeśa
he vraja-janaika-bandhu
he dineśa he prāṇeśa
rasa-rasaika-sindhu

O beloved of Rādhā! Beloved of the Vraja-gopīs and *mañjarīs*! O best friend of the Vrajavāsis! O life of the destitute and fallen! O Lord of my life! O ocean of *rasa*!

he gopeśa he rūpeśa
he vraja-vilāsi-śyāma
he gopeśvara he rāsesvara
he līlā-rasa-abhirāma

O heart of the *gopīs*! O shelter of all forms and of Śrī Rūpa! O beautiful player in the land of Vraja! O Gopesvara! O Rasesvara! O expert in playful pastimes!

he vrajanātha he prāṇanātha
he bhuvanaika-bandhu
he viśvanātha he lokanātha
he karunaika-sindhu

O Lord of Vraja and of my very life! O dearmost friend of the entire world, Lord of the universe, O ocean of mercy!

he gopinātha he rādhānātha
he śyāma-rasa-sindhu
he gopī-kānta he radha-kānta
vaṁśī-vadanānanda-indu

O Gopinātha! O Rādhānātha! O ocean of *śyāma-rasa*! O lover of the *gopīs*! Lover of Śrī Rādhā! When the full moon rose in Vraja, You stood in a three-fold bending form under the Vaṁśī-vaṭa banyan tree and attracted all the Vraja-devīs, led by Śrīmatī Rādhārānī, with the sweet call of Your flute. O Śyāma, may I always be under the guidance of those Vraja-devīs.

Contents

Introduction

Lord Caitanya Mahāprabhu offered Raghunātha dāsa Gosvāmī to Svarūpa Dāmodara. Under the shelter and guidance of Svarūpa Dāmodara, Dāsa Gosvāmī followed the process of service in Vraja.

Caitanya Mahāprabhu instructed Dāsa Gosvāmī:

amānī mānada hañā kṛṣṇa-nāma sadā la'be
vraje rādhā-kṛṣṇa-sevā mānase karibe
Caitanya-caritāmṛta, Madhya-līlā 6.237

Do not expect honor, but offer all respect to others. Always chant the holy name of Lord Kṛṣṇa, and within your mind render service to Rādhā and Kṛṣṇa in Vṛndāvana.

By sincerely chanting the holy names, while respecting all according to their position, and not being eager for respect from others, the tendency to serve Rādhā-Kṛṣṇa in Vraja shall arise. As a result of pure chanting, the Lord's form shall appear in the heart, followed by His qualities and pastimes. At that stage, absorption of the mind in Rādhā-Kṛṣṇa's pastimes will be natural, not artificial. Kṛṣṇa and His names are non-different. When one purely chants these, He will come in the heart and perform His loving pastimes with all His associates. His *līlā-śakti*, pastime potency, is always with Him. She gives the tendency and qualification to serve Kṛṣṇa.

When greed comes to serve Kṛṣṇa in one's eternal spiritual form, in time, that greed shall reveal one's eternal loving mood towards Kṛṣṇa. Then one begins to serve Kṛṣṇa under the guidance of His associates. This love matures sequentially through higher and higher degrees up to *mahābhāva*.

Nourished by transcendental nectar, or *rasa*, the soul develops its spiritual form and nature and becomes related to God.

Bhakti with a feeling of loving intimacy is dear to Kṛṣṇa. That is the only kind of worship present in Vraja. Caitanya Mahāprabhu manifested this process in the heart of Raghunātha dāsa Gosvāmī, and through him, distributed it to the world. Dāsa Gosvāmī showed by his own example how to pray for the attainment of that intimate loving mood.

This *Vilāpa-kusumāñjali* is a collection of the prayers of Dāsa Gosvāmī offered like flowers to the lotus feet of the Divine Potency of Kṛṣṇa, Śrīmatī Rādhārāṇī. By offering the heart to any mundane person, one becomes devoid of all potency and goodness. However, surrendering to Her, one attains all knowledge of Kṛṣṇa's service and becomes related to Him and His associates without any extraneous effort.

The masses emphasize more on Dāsa Gosvāmī's intense renunciation than his intimate loving mood. Indeed, evidence of the validity of Mahāprabhu's highest conception was shown in the life of Dāsa Gosvāmī as he engaged in *mānasī-sevā* in Vraja. To take Raghunātha dāsa Gosvāmī's guidance, taking shelter of his writings is essential. Then one can experience the transcendental nectar that flows through our line. If one takes shelter of this book, he will become firmly fixed in the conception and line of Mahāprabhu. This is our Guru-varga's instruction and conception.

There are two types of *anurāga—dakṣiṇa-bhāva* and *vāmya-bhāva*, right-sided and left-sided. On the left side are our Guru-varga, the followers of Śrīmatī Rādhārāṇī. But how can we collect this *anurāga* and continuously be present with it? Therefore very strong *sādhana* is necessary. If there is no strong *sādhana*, then it will not be possible to

Śrīla Raghunātha dāsa Gosvāmī

keep and preserve in your heart anything you try to catch. It will come and go; nothing will be sweet and present near you for long.

chapānna daṇḍa rātri dine
jāne nā rādhā-govinda bine
tāra para cāri daṇḍa suti thāke
svapne radhe govinda dekhe

He knows nothing but Rādhā-Govinda throughout the day and night (56 *daṇḍas*: 1 *daṇḍa* is 24 minutes). He takes rest for only 4 *daṇḍas* (1 hr. 36 min.). At that time in his dreams he receives *darśana* of Rādhā-Govinda.

The Guru-varga are serving all day long. Within the day they only take rest for one or two hours, and even as they rest they are serving in *kṛṣṇa-līlā*.

To attain such a state of spiritual rapture, we must follow the Gosvāmīs' example. This is described in the prayer:

saṅkhā-pūrvaka-nāma-gāna-natibhiḥ kālāvasānī-kṛtau
nidrāhāra-vihārakādi-vijitau cātyanta-dīnau ca yau
rādhā-kṛṣṇa-guṇa-smṛter madhurimānandena sammohitau
vande rūpa-sanātanau raghu-yugau śrī-jīva-gopālakau
Ṣaḍ-gosvāmyaṣṭakam 6

I worship the Six Gosvāmīs, who passed all their time in chanting the holy names, singing songs, and offering *daṇḍavat-praṇāma*, thereby humbly fulfilling their vow to complete a fixed number daily. In this way they utilized their valuable lives and conquered over eating and sleeping. Always seeing themselves as completely worthless, they became enchanted in divine rapture by remembering Śrī Rādhā-Kṛṣṇa's sweet qualities.

They don't have taste or relation with the body and senses. One by one they follow the process for attaining that *anurāga*. Also, if they are late for one minute in any service, then they suffer so much and repent, "Why have I lost one minute?"

They are always ready to help us attain Kṛṣṇa's mercy and the Vraja-devīs' association.

Raghunātha dāsa Gosvāmī resided in Jagannātha Purī under the guidance of Svarūpa Dāmodara, by the order of Caitanya Mahāprabhu. What did he take from Svarūpa Dāmodara? He daily collected the process of *unnata-ujjvala-rasa*. To practice this, he followed Svarūpa Dāmodara's footsteps at every moment.

He memorized and practiced what he collected from Mahāprabhu, and chanted *harināma* with intense *anurāga*.

After Mahāprabhu and Svarūpa Dāmodara disappeared, Dāsa Gosvāmī went to Vraja.

He stayed in Vṛndāvana and moved about there for sometime, but later he permanently resided at Rādhā-kuṇḍa. From morning to evening he was engaged in chanting *harināma*, while internally praying for the mercy of the Vraja-devīs and Śrīmatī Rādhārāṇī. This book is his offerings of *puṣpāñjali* to Śrīmatī Rādhārāṇī. *Puṣpāñjali* is an offering of flowers, but this book is *kusumāñjalī*, meaning, offering one's desires like heartfelt flowers. He offered his desires like this every day and at every moment. He was never disturbed, nor did he think like many others, "Is this line true?" or "Will Rādhā-Kṛṣṇa accept my prayers or not?"

His *dīkṣā-guru* is Yadunandana Ācārya, Balarāma Ācārya is his priest, and his *śikṣā-guru* is Svarūpa Dāmodara Prabhu.

Yadunandana Ācārya loved Raghunātha more than his own heart. He gave him *dīkṣā-mantra*. Haridāsa Ṭhākura, Advaita Ācārya, Nityānanda Prabhu—everyone was pleased

Śrīla Raghunātha dāsa Gosvāmī's Samadhī at Śrī Rādhā Kuṇḍa

with Raghunātha. By everyone's great mercy he followed the rules and regulations of strong *vairāgya*. His mind was never disturbed. He never followed his senses and did not give them even a little bit of time, always being busy for service of Hari, Guru and Vaiṣṇavas.

In Jagannātha Purī, Raghunātha dāsa Gosvāmī was bestowed with a special gift by Caitanya Mahāprabhu. Raghunātha dāsa Gosvāmī said, "I am a very fallen soul devoid of goodness. Nevertheless, Caitanya Mahāprabhu and Nityānanda Prabhu were very kind and merciful upon me. They offered me at the lotus feet of Svarūpa Dāmodara. And Caitanya Mahāprabhu Himself gave me a Govardhana-śilā and *guñjā-mālā*." *Guñjā-mālā* is Rādhārānī's *svarūpa*, and Śrī Govardhana is Kṛṣṇa's *svarūpa*.

Raghunātha dāsa Gosvāmī is *vairāgya-mūrti*, a personification of renunciation. It was told about him, "*Raghunāthera niyama yena pāṣāṇera rekhā*—Raghunātha dāsa Gosvāmī's *vairāgya* is as firm and resolute as lines etched in stone." It was not like one day following *bhakti's* rules, forsaking any enjoyment, and the next day thinking, "I am a great *ācārya*; taking everything is not bad for me." Raghunātha dāsa Gosvāmī did not think like this. Until his last day in this world, he followed *bhakti* strongly.

Śrī Caitanya Mahāprabhu has said:

vairāgī hañā kare jihvāra lālasa
paramārtha yāya, āra haya rasera vaśa
vairāgīra kṛtya—sadā nāma-saṅkīrtana
śāka-patra-phala-mūle udara-bharaṇa
jihvāra lālase yei iti-uti dhāya
śiśnodara-parāyaṇa kṛṣṇa nāhi pāya

Caitanya-caritāmṛta, Antya-līlā 6.225–227

> If a renunciate is eager for his tongue to taste different foods, his spiritual life will be lost, and he will be subservient to the tastes of his tongue. The duty of a person in the renounced order is to chant the Hare Kṛṣṇa *mantra* always. He should satisfy his belly with whatever vegetables, leaves, fruits and roots are available. One who is subservient to the tongue and who thus goes here and there, devoted to the genitals and the belly, cannot attain Kṛṣṇa.

One should fill his belly with whatever is easily available. By offering Kṛṣṇa foods in the mode of goodness and honoring them as *prasāda*, the tongue is satisfied and service to Kṛṣṇa is cultivated. If palatable *prasāda* is easily available, then the tongue's greed will gradually be controlled rather than increased. *Vairāgīs* continuously chant *harināma* and maintain their body with anything simple.

Raghunātha dāsa Gosvāmī never went here and there, wasting his time. He never thought, "How does salt, lemon, pickle, and chili taste?" He had deep faith and attachment. Therefore other things could never come and disturb him. His teachings and his practice were very strong. He had *bhajana-niṣṭhā* and *vairāgya*. Therefore he was always very close to the Guru-varga.

People think, "I have no fault, but the Guru-varga don't give me mercy or shelter." But they don't look at their own faults. What was Raghunātha dāsa Gosvāmī's nature? He stayed with Svarūpa Dāmodara for sixteen years continuously, and never thought, "I will go away." Why? *Vairāgya* and *bhajana-niṣṭhā* were always alive in him. Then how could he be any distance from *bhajana* and the Guru-varga? Other desires will call me and throw me out if they come, but Dāsa Gosvāmī was not like that.

He could not stay in Jagannātha Purī after Gaurahari and others disappeared—it was dry there. While there, he prayed, worshiped his Govardhana-śilā, and *guñjā-mālā*. He thought, "I shall climb on top of Govardhana and jump down, giving up my body. My separation will be finished and my heart will cool." He was crying and weeping to Jagannātha. Jagannātha gave His *prasādī-mālā* and ordered him, "Raghunātha, you are My nearest and dearest. Go to Vṛndāvana. Go to Rūpa and Sanātana and stay there."

Then he went to Vṛndāvana and wrote many prayers and instructions to the mind. In the third verse of *Manah-śikṣā*, he prays:

yadīccher āvāsaṁ vraja-bhuvi sa-rāgaṁ prati-janur
yuva-dvandvaṁ tac cet paricaritum ārād abhilaṣe
svarūpaṁ śrī-rūpaṁ sa-gaṇam iha tasyāgrajam api
sphuṭaṁ premṇā nityaṁ smara nama tadā tvaṁ śṛṇu manaḥ

> O Mind, just listen to me! If you desire to reside in Vraja birth after birth, and if you desire to directly serve the eternally youthful Divine Couple there with great attraction, then with intense love always remember and bow down to Śrīla Svarūpa Dāmodara; to Śrīla Rūpa Gosvāmī and his elder brother, Śrīla Sanātana Gosvāmī; and to all their associates and followers.

He instructed, "If you desire residence in Vraja and the service of Śrī Rādhā-Kṛṣṇa, then continuously remember and stay under the guidance of Svarūpa Dāmodara, Rūpa Gosvāmī, and Sanātana Gosvāmī. They have this *anurāga*. Follow their footsteps and stay in Vraja-dhāma. Then Govardhana, Rādhā-kuṇḍa—everyone will accept you because you followed the footsteps of the *anurāgī* devotees. Vṛndāvana-dhāma will give you all facility and chance."

He wrote *Sva-niyama Daśakam*, and there he also wrote:

gurau mantre nāmni prabhuvara-śacīgarbhaja-pade
svarūpe śrī-rūpe gaṇa-yuji tadīya-prathamaje
girīndre gāndharvā-sarasi madhu-puryāṁ vraja-vane
vraje bhakte goṣṭhālayiṣu param āstāṁ mama ratiḥ

May my *anurāga* be always with my spiritual master, the *gāyatrī-mantra,* the holy name of Lord Kṛṣṇa, Lord Caitanya Mahāprabhu's feet, Śrīla Svarūpa Dāmodara Gosvāmī, Śrīla Rūpa Gosvāmī, his associates, his elder brother (Śrīla Sanātana Gosvāmī), Govardhana Hill, Rādhā-kuṇḍa, Mathurā City, Vṛndāvana Forest, the land of Vraja, the devotees of Śrī Kṛṣṇa, and the residents of Vraja.

We come for *bhajana*, but gradually many other persons come nearby and we make a relationship with them, talk sweetly, give something and take something. They steal our hearts and take us away from Vraja-maṇḍala and the Vrajavāsīs. Therefore Dāsa Gosvāmī made a strong promise, "I will not meet, talk, accept, look, pray, or watch anything or anyone other than devotees." This was his strong *vairāgya*, naturally springing forth from his *anurāga*. He was the personification of *vairāgya* and *anurāga*. First control your own senses, your mind, and then your soul. Carefully use everything for your Gurudeva; otherwise, if you give a little share to others, they will steal you away. First they want you to be their friend, and then their slave. Then you will go very far away from transcendental *līlā*; mundane *līlā* and nature will come, and you will run for mundane tastes.

Therefore Dāsa Gosvāmī continuously followed the footsteps of Rūpa Gosvāmī and Sanātana Gosvāmī. He did not go any distance from them for one minute. Earlier, he knew nothing but Svarūpa Dāmodara and Mahāprabhu. He respected everyone, and did not talk, walk, look, watch or go to anyone. Then in

Vraja-maṇḍala, on the bank of Rādhā-kuṇḍa, he followed Rūpa and Sanātana Gosvāmī. He paid obeisance to other Vaiṣṇavas and begged them, "How can I make a sweet and strong faithful relationship with my *śikṣā-gurus*, Sanātana Gosvāmī, and Rūpa Gosvāmī."

May no doubt come. Deep faith and respect for the Vaiṣṇavas is the backbone of *bhakti*. If there is no faith in Vaiṣṇavas, then after sometime faith in *guru* and God will go away and everything will be lost.

Raghunātha dāsa Gosvāmī practiced this in his life. His heart melted and tears fell, always showering his body. Why? He was not near mundane persons; otherwise the heart will become dry like a rock. If other people steal the heart, then everything will be lost. Then no flow of love will come.

Dāsa Gosvāmī always chanted *harināma* and cried, "Hā Gauranga, hā Nityānanda, hā Svarūpa Damodara."

He composed prayers like *Śacinandana Aṣṭakam*, *Gaurāṅga Stotra*, *Svanīyama Daśakam*, *Vilāpa-kusumāñjali*, *Girirāja Govardhana Aṣṭakam*, *Rādhā-kuṇḍa Aṣṭakam*, *Śyāma-kuṇḍa Aṣṭakam*, and other prayers that spontaneously appeared in his heart. He would only sleep for four *daṇḍas*, around one and a half hours. And he used everything he possessed for service.

He would chant *harināma* while remembering *gaura-līlā*. He would remember Navadvīpa-dhāma, and from there he started his *mānasī-sevā*.

When Kavirāja Gosvāmī wrote, he always offered respect to Dāsa Gosvāmī as his *śikṣā-guru*. He also stayed at Rādhā-kuṇḍa and there he saw that Raghunātha dāsa Gosvāmī would think of Mahāprabhu's *līlā* and be engaged in *mānasī-sevā* there. Raghunātha dāsa Gosvāmī remembered Mahāprabhu's followers and how they all performed *kīrtana* together.

He remembered their glories and respectfully offered them obeisances. Then he remembered how the devotees performed *bhajana*. He prayed to them and offered *praṇāma*.

He wrote books like *Stavāvali* and *Muktā-carita*. In *Dāna-keli-cintāmaṇi*, he wrote how Kṛṣṇa takes tax from the Vraja-devīs, and what is the meaning of that tax. He wrote in *Muktā-carita* how the Vraja-devīs made Kṛṣṇa's dress with pearls and the pastimes that followed.

Out of his many books, this *Vilāpa-kusumāñjali* is especially important. Everyday he prayed with these verses, offering flowers to Rādhārāṇī's lotus feet. He wrote:

devi duḥkha kula-sāgarodare
dūyamāna mati durgataṁ janaṁ
tvat kṛpā pravala naukayādbhutaṁ
prāpaya svapada-paṅka-jālayam

Vilāpa-kusumāñjali 17

O Goddess, please rescue this unfortunate person drowning in the ocean of unhappiness. Place me in the strong boat of Your mercy and carry me to the shore of Your lotus feet.

He wrote these verses, internally feeling as if he was burning in a heat fiercer than millions of fires combined. Why does he cry and weep so? This is *prema-vilāpa*. When love is very deep, the separation also becomes very deep. What is this language and mood? No one can understand.

In his perfected condition, Dāsa Gosvāmī is a *pālya-dāsī*, following the footsteps of Lalitā-devī and serving Vṛndāvana-vilāsinī Śrīmatī Rādhārāṇī.

He wrote *Vraja-vilāsa-stava* when he was advanced in age. He prayed, "Oh! Now I am old and my body is not helpful for Your service. The snake of time has bitten me, sapping all my energy. Now he is trying to steal me and keep me away from You.

But no, no, no, I am not old; I am young; I am the follower of Your beloved. *He* Svāminī, without Your *darśana* and service I can't feel well for even a moment. Therefore continuously give me Your service—this is my only desire. May I continuously serve You in my *kiśorī* age in this Vṛndāvana-dhāma. *He* Rūpa Mañjarī, your service tendency and mood runs on incessantly. I will learn that process and will continuously follow it. Therefore give me eyes. May I not watch other things. I will learn only the rules and regulations of this line."

Dāsa Gosvāmī forgot his own external body and prayed only for Rādhārāṇī's *dāsyam*:

tavaivāsmi tavaivāsmi na jīvāmi tvayā vinā
iti vijñāya devi tvaṁ naya māṁ caraṇāntike

I am Yours! I am Yours! I cannot live without You. O Śrī Rādhe, knowing this, please give me a place at Your lotus feet.

While instructing his own mind, He also prayed:

yathā duṣṭatvaṁ me davayati śaṭhasyāpi kṛpayā
yathā mahyaṁ premāmṛtam api dadāty ujjvalam asau
yathā śrī gāndharvā-bhajana-vidhaye prerayati māṁ
tathā goṣṭhe kākvā giridharam iha tvaṁ bhaja manaḥ

Manaḥ-śikṣā 8

O mind, with utter humility and grief-stricken words, just worship Śrī Giridhārī-Kṛṣṇa in Vraja in such a way that He will become pleased with me. By His causeless mercy He will remove my wickedness, bestow the nectar of His supremely radiant love, and confer upon me the inspiration to worship Śrīmatī Rādhikā.

He prayed, "O my dear mind. You are very naughty and stupid. You take me far away from Girirāja Govardhana.

O Girirāja Govardhana, I pray to you. Defeat my mind, kick away anyone who comes near me, and protect me. I will not try to go away from Rādhārānī's service for even one second. I do not want to go away from the guidance of Rūpa Mañjarī. I will serve under the guidance of Rūpa Mañjarī and Guṇa Mañjarī. When will that *rati*, love, come to me?"

He prayed to the lotus feet of Rādhārānī for Her service:

pādābjayos tava vinā vara dāsyam eva
nānyat kadāpi samaye kila devi yāce
sākhyāya te mama namo 'stu namo 'stu nityaṁ
dāsyāya te mama raso 'stu raso 'stu satyam

O Devī Rādhike! I never desire anything but the best loving service unto Your lotus feet. If You want to give me the position of a *sakhī*, then I offer my obeisances again and again to that position from a distance, but I do not actually want it. Taking a vow, I am begging only to have steadfast *anurāga* in Your service.

He prayed, "*He* Devī, there is no need for Your friendship, only for *dāsya*. I don't want the position of a friend, I only desire to serve You."

In *Svanīyama-daśakam* (Verse 6) he prayed:

anādṛtyodgītām api muni-gaṇair vaiṇika-mukhaiḥ
pravīṇāṁ gāndharvām api ca nigamais tat-priyatamām
ya ekaṁ govindaṁ bhajati kapaṭī dāmbhikatayā
tad-abhyarṇe śīrṇe kṣaṇam api na yāmi vratam idam

Not for a moment shall I go near a hypocrite who worships only Lord Govinda and does not worship exalted Śrīmatī Rādhārāṇī, who is glorified by the Vedas and the great sages headed by Nārada, and who is most dear to Ṣrī Kṛṣṇa. This is my vow.

Śrīla Bhaktivinoda Ṭhākura sings:

nārada muni, bājāya vīṇā, 'rādhikā-ramana'
name, nāma amani udita hoya, bhakata-gīta-sāme

When the great soul Nārada Muni plays his stringed *vīṇā*, the holy name of Rādhikā-ramaṇa descends and immediately appears amidst the *kīrtana* of the Lord's devotees.

śrī-kṛṣṇa-nāma rasane sphuri' pūrā'lo āmāra āśa
śrī-rūpa-pade yācaye ihā bhakativinoda-dāsa

The holy name of Śrī Kṛṣṇa has fulfilled all my desires by thus manifesting on everyone's tongue. Bhaktivinoda, the humble servant of the Lord, therefore prays at the feet of Śrī Rūpa Gosvāmī that the chanting of *harināma* may always continue in this way.

Nārada Ṛṣi sweetly sings the holy names of Govinda; by Rādhārāṇī's mercy he cannot forget Kṛṣṇa's names. Without the mercy of Śrīmatī Rādhārāṇī it is not possible for anyone to chant, sing, pray and be present in Vraja near the Vrajavāsīs. Otherwise he gets the mercy of *māyā*—he will explain and remember *māyā's* qualities; he will serve her. The mercy of *svarūpa-śakti* is necessary.

Inside this *Vilāpa-kusumāñjali*, Dāsa Gosvāmī prays for *rādhā-niṣṭhā*. He taught everyone *vairāgya* and *bhajana*, and the process to achieve *vraja-sevā* and the blessings of *svarūpa-śakti* and the Vraja-devīs. Gurudeva brings a flow of *rasa* like a river. He arranges and keeps this. If anyone showers in it, then he is very lucky. This is a river, not a lake, meaning, this *rasa* is continuously flowing. In *Vilāpa-kusumāñjali*, *Stavāvali* and other books, Dāsa Gosvāmī brought this flow. If anyone bathes in or drinks this, he will be attracted to *svarūpa-śakti* and come close to Her. He will never wander away from Her. This is the best process as told by Raghunātha dāsa Gosvāmī. After learning this, we will attain some greed for *sādhana*.

tvaṁ rūpa-mañjari sakhi! prathitā pure 'smin
puṁsaḥ parasya vadanaṁ na hi paśyasīti
bimbādhare kṣatam anāgata-bhartṛkāyā
yat te vyadhāyi kim u tac chuka-puṅgavena
Vilāpa-kusumāñjali 1

My dear *sakhī* Rūpa Mañjarī, you are well known in Vraja for not even looking at the face of any man other than your husband. Therefore it is surprising that your lips, red like *bimba* fruits, have been bitten, even though your husband is not at home. Has this been done by the best of parrots?

On October 21st, 1992, Śrīla Gurudeva spoke on this first verse of *Vilāpa-kusumāñjali* in a *darśana* with Tamal Kṛṣṇa Mahārāja and other ISKCON *sannyāsīs*. Śrīla Gurudeva said:

Was Raghunātha dāsa Gosvāmī weeping or laughing? It may seem that he wrote this verse in a laughing, pleasant mood. Actually, however, he was remembering a previous pastime and weeping at the feet of Śrī Rūpa Mañjarī, "You have been so merciful to me. I remember seeing your mood after Kṛṣṇa kissed you and left a mark on your lips. When will I see you in that condition again?" In the second *śloka*, *sthala-kamalini yuktaṁ*, he is again offering *praṇāma* and weeping, "Will I see this again?" These first two verses are very important.

Raghunātha dāsa Gosvāmī starts this book advising us to follow *rāga-mārga*. This prayer is helpful for everyone.

One who does not want to cross over this material ocean should not read this book. On the other hand, one who desires to follow the process of *rāgānuga-bhakti* and achieve *kṛṣṇa-prema* and *rādhā-dāsyam* will regularly pray with these verses of *Vilāpa-kusumāñjali* and will keep this book close to his heart like a cherished friend and guardian.

Guru-Vaiṣṇava kṛpā-leṣa prārthi,
Rasik Mohan dāsa
Giridhari dāsa
Kṛṣṇa-karunyā dāsa
and all others...

1

A Glimpse of Guru's Glory and Mercy

How can we come close to the Gosvāmīs? How can we make a relationship with them and follow their footsteps if we have no knowledge of the process of *rāgānuga-bhakti*? One's own imagination and speculation is not *bhakti*. To follow the rules and regulations of *rāgānuga-bhakti*, following Raghunātha dāsa Gosvāmī's footsteps is necessary. In Caitanya Mahāprabhu's time he was with Svarūpa Dāmodara, and in his eternal form he is engaged in his eternally perfect service, under the guidance of Śrī Rūpa Mañjarī. He wrote, prayed for, and reserved this process of *rāgānuga* and *rūpānuga-bhakti* for us all. This is very helpful for all *sādhakas*, especially those in Mahāprabhu's line. In Mahāprabhu's line, *vaidhī-bhakti* does not have so much value. The *sādhana* process of *rāgānuga-bhakti* is necessary to learn and follow. If you don't understand it or feel you have no *adhikāra*, no problem. Everyone's heart has *anurāga*, love; when this is misused, one suffers. By *vaidhī-bhakti* one can't bring this love back; there will be only some control, and one cannot gain entrance and position in Vraja-maṇḍala. By following the process of *anurāgamayī-bhakti*, by slowly using this *anurāga* under the guidance of the Gosvāmīs, and following the Vraja-devīs' footsteps, this *anurāga* comes back, and then there is no more problem.

Therefore, without *adhikāra*, if anyone insults, taunts or says anything against this, then it is their own idea and speculation. *Śāstra* doesn't teach like this. Babies don't know etiquette; even without taste they go to school, sent by their parents, and gradually, a little taste comes and then they follow everything by themselves. Similarly, if we don't follow the Gosvāmīs' footsteps, who will we follow? Will we go to ordinary conditioned souls? Will we then progress in life and get purification and clearance?

Who will help us for *ceto-darpaṇa-mārjanam*, cleansing the mirror of the heart? People place a ban on conditioned souls, "Don't go forward and cross *vaidhī-mārga*; don't try to enter *rāgānuga-mārga*; you have no *adhikāra*."

How can *adhikāra* come? I think these people are very cruel, hard cheaters. They always punish the *jīvas*, "Don't go, don't follow, don't look." Then who is helpful? If we don't follow our Gosvāmīs and Guru-varga's footsteps, advice, and orders, then how can we cross *māyā*? Therefore we chant, read, and move here and there for a long time, following the wrong footsteps, until we finally give up and run, jumping into the lap of *māyā*, unable to cross *māyā*. Why is this? Only because we don't follow our Guru-varga and Gosvāmīs. Therefore, don't doubt this process of *rāgānuga-bhakti*. This *bhakti* is very sweet, easy, favorable, helpful and natural. The *jīvas* naturally have love for God, but because of bad association they misuse this. In this world people teach so many things, such as, "Controlling your love is good. Renounce everything. This world is illusory." But after that, what will they do? How can one use this love permanently for its proper object?

Those who teach mere negation have no idea of the positive truth. Therefore we offer respect and *puṣpāñjali* to *vaidhī-bhakti-marga*, and leaving it on one side, we follow the Gosvāmīs' footsteps.

ei chaya gosāi jabe vraje kailā vāsa
rādhā-kṛṣṇa-nitya-līlā karilā prakāśa

When the Six Gosvāmīs lived in Vraja they revealed the pastimes of Rādhā and Kṛṣṇa.

These Gosvāmīs discovered the eternal pastimes of Rādhā-Kṛṣṇa in Vṛndāvana and gave them to the conditioned souls.

ei chaya gosāi kori caraṇa vandana
jāhā hoite vighna-nāśa abhīṣṭa-pūraṇa

By the causeless mercy of the Six Gosvāmīs the obstacles to devotion can be removed and my *abhīṣṭa* Śrī Yugala-sevā can be attained, that is, all my desires can be fulfilled.

By following the Gosvāmīs' footsteps, all disturbances and obstacles are destroyed. Then why don't we follow the Gosvāmīs? By force people press others, hiding themselves in the darkness. They say to others, "Oh, stay with me in this dark and deep well; don't come out; don't look towards the light." They try to make you lazy, crazy, and intoxicated, giving you wine and beer to make you paralyzed day and night in a room, as if you are in a coma. This is not human life!

This is not the process to awaken the soul. How can we awaken the soul's love and affection for the Supreme Soul? The Gosvāmīs teach this by their example. If we don't follow this then we will engage in foolish activities.

We should pray, "How can I attain my true service? How can I learn and go close to the Gosvāmīs, Guru-varga, and Vraja-devīs?" This process must be followed very strictly—then I am a *sādhaka;* then I am in the Guru-varga's line and am their follower.

In the first *śloka*, Raghunātha dāsa Gosvāmī offers *maṅgalācaraṇa*. The rule is to first offer *maṅgalācaraṇa* for some auspiciousness and prayer. But to whom? To *guru*. If *guru* is pleased, then everything is good. Everything is for *guru's* satisfaction.

How do you offer *praṇāma* in our *rūpānuga-marga*? In *vaidhi-mārga* worship is done with *pādya, ācamana, puṣpāñjali, arghya, āsana, madhuparka*, and so forth, but *rāgānuga-bhakti* is not like this. Raghunātha dāsa Gosvāmī offers *praṇāma*:

> *tvaṁ rūpa-mañjari sakhi! prathitā pure 'smin*
> *puṁsaḥ parasya vadanaṁ na hi paśyasīti*
> *bimbādhare kṣatam anāgata-bhartṛkāyā*
> *yat te vyadhāyi kim u tac chuka-puṅgavena*
>
> *Vilāpa-kusumāñjali* 1

My dear *sakhī* Rūpa Mañjarī, you are well known in Vraja for not even looking at the face of any man other than your husband. Therefore it is surprising that your lips, red like *bimba* fruits, have been bitten, even though your husband is not at home. Has this been done by the best of parrots?

Raghunātha dāsa Gosvāmī offers *praṇāma* to Rūpa Gosvāmī. How? Not by touching his feet, taking *caraṇāmṛta*, and doing *parikramā* ten times. What does Dāsa Gosvāmī Prabhu say? While praying, Dāsa Gosvāmī Prabhu remembers his own internal service and perceives a vision of Vraja's pastimes. He sees: "Rūpa Mañjarī is present in Vraja-maṇḍala? She is very honest and chaste; she never watches any gentleman. She is always with Śrīmatī Rādhārāṇī. She is Śrīmatī Rādhārāṇī's nearest and dearest *mañjarī*."

Dāsa Gosvāmī looked at Rūpa Mañjarī's face. He didn't look at her feet; he looked at her face and saw that it appeared someone had bitten her lips, leaving a red mark. Observing this, he thought, "What is the matter? Who came? And from where and how? What type of parrot has come, and, as if attracted by the fragrance of a ripe fruit, bit into the fruit and taken some juice? Rūpa Mañjarī is very close and dear to Rādhārāṇī, and is full of the flow of *rasa* coming from Her.

With this she serves Rādhārānī. But who came and tasted her, and then ran away?"

Here Dāsa Gosvāmī teaches how one offers proper *praṇāma* to Guru-pāda-padma in the *rāgānugā-mārga*. *Guru-stuti* and *guru-pūjā* are necessary. Who gives Rādhārānī's *mantra*? Who gives advice to chant and remember this? This is given by Śrīla Gurudeva.

Dāsa Gosvāmī Prabhu prays to Rūpa Gosvāmī Prabhu in his *siddha-avasthā*, perfected state. Dāsa Gosvāmī understood that Rādhārānī sent Kṛṣṇa in the early morning, "Go to Rūpa Mañjarī. Day and night she is continuously serving, pleasing and helping Me. She is honest and never meets or speaks with anyone else; she doesn't even look at any other; she doesn't know anything except My service. Go to her."

If the disciple has a deep relation with his *guru*, then he can understand how much love his *guru* has for Kṛṣṇa, and how much love Kṛṣṇa has for his *guru*. One can then understand how much Kṛṣṇa likes Rūpa Mañjarī, how near and dear she is to Him, and how Śrīmatī Rādhārānī is pleased with her. Therefore She sends Kṛṣṇa, "Kṛṣṇa! Don't you know this Rūpa Mañjarī? Why don't You go and give her some of Your love and affection?"

Everything may be ready, but if Kṛṣṇa doesn't accept it, that is not called *prasāda*. Anything that Kṛṣṇa accepts becomes His *prasāda*, and then it is helpful for everyone.

The *sādhaka* must pray and remember his Guru-pāda-padma. Guru-pāda-padma is a *siddha*, eternally perfected *mahā-bhāgavata*. From his heart, blessings will come, and then the *sādhaka* will see his own *siddha-svarūpa*, Guru-pāda-padma's *siddha-svarūpa*, and Guru-pāda-padma's service and specialties. He will understand this and become greedy for spiritual service. This greed is essential. If there is no spiritual greed, then *bhakti* will never, never increase.

So with this first *śloka*, Raghunātha dāsa Gosvāmī offers *praṇāma* to Rūpa Gosvāmī in his eternal form as Rūpa Mañjarī, remembering the blessings of Kṛṣṇa for her.

It is not possible that without Rādhārānī's instruction Kṛṣṇa would go and kiss and bite the lips of Rūpa Mañjarī. This is not possible. Why? Kṛṣṇa is not independent of Rādhārāṇī.

Rūpa Mañjarī also isn't waiting for this love from Kṛṣṇa. But Śrīmatī Rādhārāṇī knows how to distribute Kṛṣṇa's love and blessings to everyone. Therefore Her arrangement is good.

sthala-kamalini yuktaṁ garvitā kānane 'smin
praṇayasi vara-hāsyaṁ puṣpa-guccha-cchalena
api nikhila-latās tāḥ saurabhāktaḥ sa muñcan
mṛgayati tava mārgaṁ kṛṣṇa-bhṛṅgo yad adya

Vilāpa-kusumāñjali 2

O lotus tree, on the pretext of this bunch of new blossoms you are now broadly smiling in this forest. You have every right to be proud. After all, the black Kṛṣṇa-bee has left all the fragrant flower-vines and He is now searching for the pathway to you.

A lotus generally blossoms in the water, in any river or lake, but here it is told that there is a garden in which a wonderful lotus has blossomed without the need of any water body. This sacred place is Vṛndā-devī's garden. Who is this lotus? Rūpa Mañjarī. She is more wonderful than millions of lotuses. Her fragrance, color, beauty, nature—everything is millions of times greater than lotuses.

The special qualities of Guru-pāda-padma appear in the hearts of his perfected followers. Otherwise disciples pray and offer *praṇāma* with mundane ideas and words without understanding their Gurudeva's actual position.

Here Raghunātha dāsa Gosvāmī says, "In this garden there is one lotus who is very proud of her good fortune. There are many other flowers in the garden, yet today the famous black bumblebee of Vraja has left all others and come to relish this lotus."

There were many other flowers there, like other *mañjarīs* and *sakhīs*, but Śrīmatī Rādhārāṇī exclaimed, "Oh! How is this flower!" Rādhārāṇī laughed and went to this lotus, but not alone—She was followed by one black bumblebee. Kṛṣṇa is very greedy. He is like a bumblebee that goes to drink honey from the lotuses in lakes. But today He saw that there is a lotus in the garden from which a very sweet aroma was coming. This fragrance was very attractive and strong. He ran, maddened by this fragrance, looking, "Where did this lotus come from? This is very attractive, sweet and beautiful, with such nice color." Now Kṛṣṇa was restless, but how could He touch and take the lotus? He has this desire. He hid amongst the *sakhīs* and went nearby Śrīmatī Rādhārāṇī. Then Rādhārāṇī called forth Rūpa Mañjarī.

Rūpa Mañjarī came forward, her beautiful face smiling, a little proud of her fortune.

"Just look how wonderful this flower is!" Rādhārāṇī indicated to Kṛṣṇa. "Smell and look at this flower. You have never seen such a lotus blossomed in this garden before! Look at this lotus and smell the fragrance, but don't pick or take the lotus and run away with her!" Then Rādhārāṇī departed to another *kuñja*.

Kṛṣṇa hovered from this side to that side like a bumblebee, and then suddenly caught Rūpa Mañjarī and kissed her lips. Astonished, Rūpa Mañjarī ran away very quickly, not staying there a moment longer. She is very honest and chaste. She thought, "How could Kṛṣṇa come, touch, and contaminate me!" She then ran to another *kuñja*. Kṛṣṇa tried to follow her, but she ran very fast to Rādhārāṇī and hid under Her *cādara*. Then Kṛṣṇa could no longer come near her. It was like He had lost something very valuable. He lamented, "Why did I go to touch and disturb her? This is not good. Now everyone will reject Me. No one will give Me entrance again. They will never speak to Me or take My name again. Now I have been rejected!"

He went far away and sat under a *kadamba* tree, casting His flute to one side. He sat and thought, "What can I do? I see no solution. I am very greedy, a *lampaṭa*. I don't know what process to follow. Rādhā only told Me to look at the flower, smell it and come back, but I tried to pick the flower and run with it. I did this thief business and am therefore suffering."

When the *sādhaka* meets with *guru* in his *siddha-svarūpa*, then he realizes the position of Guru-pāda-padma—how he is serving, how he is near and dear to Śrīmatī Rādhārāṇī, and how Kṛṣṇa is greedy to have some sweet interaction with him.

Now Kṛṣṇa waited and thought, "When will I next get the good fortune to once address her? If she tells me something, and I hear one or two words from her, this is good for me."

But Rūpa Mañjarī never goes out and does anything independently of Śrīmatī Rādhārāṇī. Why? Rūpa Gosvāmī instructed:

anyābhilāṣitā-śūnyaṁ jñāna-karmādy-anāvṛtam
ānukūlyena kṛṣṇānu-śīlanaṁ bhaktir uttamā

Bhakti-rasāmṛta-sindhu 1.1.11

The cultivation of activities that are meant exclusively for the pleasure of Śrī Kṛṣṇa, or in other words the uninterrupted flow of service to Śrī Kṛṣṇa, performed through all endeavors of the body, mind and speech, and through the expression of various spiritual sentiments (*bhāvas*), which is not covered by *jñāna* (knowledge aimed at impersonal liberation) and *karma* (reward-seeking activity), and which is devoid of all desires other than the aspiration to bring happiness to Śrī Kṛṣṇa, is called pure devotional service.

The word *kṛṣṇānuśīlanam* may either be read as *kṛṣṇā-anuśīlanam* or *kṛṣṇa-anuśīlanam.* Kṛṣṇā means Rādhā and *anuśilanam* means to follow. What is proper—*kṛṣṇā-anuśīlanam* or *kṛṣṇa-anuśīlanam,* following Rādhārāṇī or Kṛṣṇa? If there is *kṛṣṇa-anuśīlanam* under the guidance of Rādhārāṇī, then that is perfect. Otherwise if one tries to please Kṛṣṇa without Rādhārāṇī's permission and guidance, anything he does would be improper.

Rūpa Mañjarī doesn't independently go near Kṛṣṇa, meet with Him, serve Him or do anything; she is solely surrendered to Rādhārāṇī. This is called *guru-anugatya.*

Many people came and took *dīkṣā* and *harināma,* and Gurudeva told them to serve God's Deities. Then they run to serve God's Deities but do nothing for Guru-pāda-padma; they don't serve him and have no relation with him. Everything must first be offered to Śrīla Gurudeva. It is the disciple's duty to offer everything to Śrīla Gurudeva. Guru checks whether the disciple's offering is right or wrong, perfect or not. If everything is sweet, perfect, favorable, and tasteful, then what I offer will be given by Śrīla Gurudeva to his senior, meaning, from *guru* it will be offered to *param-guru,* to *parātpara-guru,* and all the way up to Rūpa Mañjarī, to Lalitā, Viśākhā, and Rādhārāṇī, and then after being checked by Rādhārāṇī this goes to Kṛṣṇa.

Now people jump and run, saying, "Gurudeva told me to do this. I am now a great devotee. I will try to please Kṛṣṇa and Rādhārāṇī with my own big idea and understanding." This is nothing; this is zero! After sometime one will have no taste and will run away from service; he will not serve Rādhā-Govinda and Rādhā-Kṛṣṇa, rather he will serve mundane ladies and babies. This is mundane nature. Why do they run away? They are not attached to Śrī Guru.

But what is the nature of Rūpa Mañjarī? Kṛṣṇa left everyone and searched for Rūpa Mañjarī. Why? Because she is the nearest and dearest of Rādhārānī.

If Rādhārānī has affection for anyone, She will not be fully pleased unless Her beloved, Kṛṣṇa, has shown affection to that person. For example: if I have affection for you, and Gurudeva shows you affection, then it will please me very much. Like this, Rādhārānī desired that Kṛṣṇa show affection to Rūpa Mañjarī. By this She is very pleased. Kṛṣṇa went near Rūpa Mañjarī for the happiness of Rādhārānī.

Rūpa Mañjarī ran away because she did not want to independently accept any affection from Kṛṣṇa. This is the nature of her love. Rūpa Mañjarī is extremely close to Śrīmatī Rādhārānī, like Her own beloved expansion. Her very form is so similar to Rādhārānī's that Kṛṣṇa sometimes cannot distinguish between the two.

Kṛṣṇa is in Rādhārānī's heart, and Rādhārānī is in Rūpa Mañjarī's heart. When Kṛṣṇa went forward to Rūpa Mañjarī, He saw, 'Only Rādhārānī is present here.' Did Kṛṣṇa make a mistake, or was His perception the truth? He became perplexed, "Who is this?" From top to bottom, inside and without, Rūpa Mañjarī is the embodiment of Rādhārānī. She has place for no other. So Kṛṣṇa did not make a mistake.

Kṛṣṇa could not understand clearly, "Who is this? Is it Rūpa or Rādhārānī?" When Kṛṣṇa looked at Rūpa, He only saw Rādhārānī. It says in *Caitanya-caritāmṛta* (*Madhya-līlā* 8.274):

sthāvara-jaṅgama dekhe, nā dekhe tāra mūrti
sarvatra haya nija iṣṭa-deva-sphūrti

The *mahā-bhāgavata* certainly sees everything animate and inanimate, but he does not exactly see their forms. Rather, everywhere he looks, he immediately sees the manifest form of his worshipable Lord.

Kṛṣṇa comes to Rādhā-kuṇḍa and in all the creepers, plants, trees, and objects around Rādhā-kuṇḍa, He sees only the manifold *svarūpas* of Rādhārāṇī. Whatever picture of Rādhārāṇī these beings keep in their heart, those dancing images of Rādhārāṇī come as a reflection in Kṛṣṇa's eyes. Seeing this, Kṛṣṇa becomes astonished and begins to dance in joy.

Vṛndā-devī comes to Kṛṣṇa and asks Him, "What are You doing?"

"I am learning how to dance."

"Who is Your *guru*."

"Rādhārāṇī in all the plants and creepers around Rādhā-kuṇḍa."

rādhikāra prema-guru, āmi śiṣya naṭa
sadā āmā nānā nṛtye nācāya udbhaṭa
Śrī Caitanya-caritāmṛta, Ādi-līlā 4.124

Śrī Kṛṣṇa says, "The love of Rādhikā is My teacher, and I am Her dancing pupil. Her *prema* makes Me dance various novel dances."

Like this, Kṛṣṇa went to Rūpa Mañjarī and, becoming bewildered, He kissed her, thinking she was Rādhārāṇī. Kṛṣṇa saw that within and without, Rūpa Mañjarī was the embodiment of Rādhārāṇī. He became confused, and thought, "Who is this? Is it Rādhārāṇī?" There is no one else who is so absorbed in Rādhārāṇī that she has become like Rādhārāṇī's second form.

Rādhārāṇī had desire for Kṛṣṇa to give affection to Rūpa Mañjarī, therefore Kṛṣṇa went near Rūpa, but He became bewildered seeing her, not understanding if it was Rādhārānī or Rūpa Mañjarī.

Raghunātha dāsa Gosvāmī saw that Kṛṣṇa went to Rūpa. Why? Hear one thing. Kṛṣṇa always kisses Rādhārānī, not merely once. But then what is the specialty here for Rūpa Mañjarī? This prayer by Raghunātha dāsa Gosvāmī describes Rūpa Mañjarī's specialty.

Kṛṣṇa is always with Rādhārānī and enjoys pastimes with Her, but when He goes to Rūpa Mañjarī it shows Rūpa's specialty.

In the *Arcana-dīpikā*, it is said:

rādhā-sammukha-saṁsaktiṁ
sakhī-saṅga-nivāsinīm
tvām ahaṁ satataṁ vande
mādhavāśraya-vigrahām

O Gurudeva, I continually offer my obeisances unto you, who are always in the presence of Srīmatī Rādhārāṇī and are very devoted to Her. You always reside in the association of Her confidantes, the *gopīs*, and you are the abode of loving devotion to Śrī Mādhava.

This is *guru-vandanā* and *stuti*. How many things are indicated here? You don't know this. One day Śrīla Gurudeva pulled me after *ārati*, and sending out all others, asked me in his room, "Hey, do you know the meaning of *krsnānandāya-dhīmahi*?

"What do I know?" I replied.

"*Kṛṣṇānanda* means that Śrī Guru gives *ānanda* to Kṛṣṇa," Śrīla Gurudeva said. "It also refers to Rādhārānī, who is known as Kṛṣṇā."

How does Gurudeva give *ānanda* to Rādhā-Kṛṣṇa? How does he serve? How near is he to the Divine Couple?

nikuñja-yūno rati-keli-siddhyai
yā yālibhir yuktir apekṣanīyā
tatrāti-dākṣyād ati-vallabhasya
vande guroḥ śrī caraṇāravindam

Śrī Gurvāṣṭakam 6

Śrī Gurudeva is always present with the *sakhīs,* planning the arrangements for the perfection of *yugala-kiśora's* amorous pastimes (*rati-keli*) within the *kuñjas* of Vṛndāvana. Because he is so expert in making these tasteful arrangements for Their pleasure, he is very dear to Śrī Rādhā and Kṛṣṇa. I offer prayers unto the lotus feet of Śrī Gurudeva.

The *rūpānuga-guru* is most expert at serving in the confidential pastimes of Rādhā-Kṛṣṇa. How does he serve? *Kṛṣṇānanda* means *sevānanda.* By doing service, Kṛṣṇa is pleased. What is that service? When you go near *guru* in reality, then you will be able to understand these topics. The *mañjarīs* only desire, "How can I arrange Rādhārāṇī's meeting with Kṛṣṇa?" None of the *mañjarīs* have any separate desire to meet with Kṛṣṇa.

vrajendra-vasati-sthale vividha-ballavī-saṅkule
tvam eva rati-mañjari pracura-puṇya-puñjodayā
vilāsa-bhara-vismṛta-praṇayi-mekhalā-mārgaṇe
yad adya nija-nāthayā vrajasi nāthitā kandaram

Vilāpa-kusumāñjali 3

O Rati Mañjarī, in the king of Vraja's city, where many *gopīs* live, you are the most pious of all. That is why you are now going to a cave, requested by your queen, to search for the favorite sash of bells She forgot in the midst of many pastimes.

Aho! Now, in the *kuñja-kuṭīra*, Kṛṣṇa came to search for Rūpa Mañjarī, but He couldn't find her. Why? She had gone and hidden under Rādhārāṇī's shawl. Kṛṣṇa chanted and remembered her name, searching for her in the *kuñja*. Then He saw that Rūpa Mañjarī was not inside the *kuñja*. There was another *mañjarī*.

"Who is she?" He wondered.

Her head was covered with a peacock-feather colored shawl. Kṛṣṇa ran forward and lifted up this shawl a little bit and looked into her face.

"Who is this new one who has come in the *kuñja*?" He thought. Her name is Rati Mañjarī.

At the time of perfecting one's *bhajana*, one goes to Vraja-maṇḍala in one's eternal *siddha-svarūpa*, with a desire for service. Rādhārāṇī gives some blessing, which comes through Rūpa Mañjarī, to Rati Mañjarī, through the *mañjarīs* to Gurudeva and then to the perfected disciples.

We must be firm in our dedication: "I will follow close in Śrīla Gurudeva's footsteps. He gave *harināma* and *dīkṣā*. I will chant these in *brāhma-muhūrta* and be with him. Then automatically his heart will melt and a flow of mercy and inspiration will come in my heart."

Now Kṛṣṇa saw that Rati Mañjarī had come.

"Bring My shawl," Rādhārāṇī had told Rati Mañjarī. She walked through the inner *kuñja* and came outside, where Kṛṣṇa met her.

"Do you know Rūpa Mañjarī?" He asked. "Where is she? How can I meet with her?" He was very greedy. "Please help me just once. I want to ask for forgiveness. What I did was improper. She is very honest and chaste. I promise not to disturb her anymore. Let her know that I pray she may one day be pleased with Me."

Rati Mañjarī went inside a cave without answering. Without the permission of Śrīmatī Rādhārāṇī, she didn't speak or look at Kṛṣṇa.

Rati Mañjarī is Raghunātha dāsa Gosvāmī. Some say that Raghunātha dāsa Gosvāmī is Rasa Mañjarī or Tulasī Mañjarī. Vaiṣṇavas see according to their own position. However, our Śrīla Gurudeva describes that Raghunātha dāsa Gosvāmī in his *siddha-svarūpa* serves the Divine Couple as Rati Mañjarī.

If anyone follows *rāgamayī-sevā*, then Kṛṣṇa Himself will come thousands of times to that person. There will be no need to take shelter of any other process to please Him; He will automatically be very pleased.

Dāsa Gosvāmī prays:

prabhur api yadunandano ya eṣa
priya-yadunandana unnata-prabhavaḥ
svayam atula-kṛpāmṛtābhiṣekaṁ
mama kṛtavaṁs tam ahaṁ guruṁ prapadye

Vilāpa-kusumāñjali 4

Let me surrender to my spiritual master, Yadunandana Ācārya. Being a powerful and dear devotee of the Supreme Lord, he sprinkled the nectar of his mercy upon me.

"One Yadunandana is Kṛṣṇa, but His nearest and dearest, my beloved Guru-pāda-padma, is also named Yadunandana. He is the embodiment of Kṛṣṇa's mercy; therefore, he is my *guru*. I took shelter of him and he also accepted me. He offered me to the lotus feet of Mahāprabhu, made my relation with Svarūpa Dāmodara, and gave me service under guidance of Rūpa Gosvāmī."

Kṛṣṇa-mantra is given by *dīkṣā-guru*, and *śikṣā-guru* teaches *vraja-bhakti* or *rāgānuga-bhakti*. Sometimes *dīkṣā-guru* also accepts the position of *śikṣā-guru*. With respect to *dīkṣā-guru*, the disciple has a mood of awe and reverence, but *śikṣā-guru* is like one's dear friend, with him everything can be openly discussed. If one disrespects *dīkṣā-guru*, that is a great problem in the life of a *sādhaka*, but *śikṣā-guru* is always helping and is not disturbed if one perchance misbehaves.

A mother always takes care of her babies. If babies are angry and sometimes break or destroy things, their mother is never angry with them. This is a mundane example. *Śikṣā-guru*, however, is millions of times more kind than a mother.

Raghunātha dāsa Gosvāmī now glorifies his *dīkṣā-guru*, Yadunandana Ācārya: "My Guru Mahārāja took me out of *māyā*; he gave me power to renounce all material things. If my Guru-pāda-padma did not accept me, I couldn't have given up anything. My body is with me since millions of lives and I am very attached to it. Because of my Guru-pāda-padma's mercy and power, I had no taste or attachment to my beautiful young wife, wealth, or anything. After that, so much respect followed me, but Gurudeva protected me; he always gave a strong boundary so that nothing could come inside and disturb me. If Guru-pāda-padma didn't protect me, then I could never progress."

In the fifth verse, Raghunātha dāsa Gosvāmī prays:

yo māṁ dustara-geha-nirjala-mahā-kūpād apāra-klamāt
sadyaḥ sāndra-dayāmbudhiḥ prakṛtitaḥ svairī kṛpā-rajjubhiḥ
uddhṛtyātma-saroja-nindi-caraṇa-prāntaṁ prapadya svayaṁ
śrī-dāmodara-sac-cakāra tam ahaṁ caitanyacandraṁ bhaje

> I worship Lord Caitanya-candra, the supremely independent ocean of mercy, who with His ropes of mercy quickly lifted me from the endlessly troublesome dry well of household life, from which escape is very difficult, who gave me the shelter of His feet which rebuke the beauty of lotuses, and who gave me to Svarūpa Dāmodara Gosvāmī.

Who understands the glories of Śrīla Gurudeva? If someone sends a poor helpless person to school, maintains him in every way, and takes care of him attentively, then when he becomes a post graduate, and thereafter a minister, he thinks, "This person was so kind to me. I was a poor orphan with no helper; I was suffering in the street and no one gave me one drop of water or food, but that person always helped me."

Similarly, if anyone crosses *māyā*, he will be somewhat able to understand the glories of Guru-pāda-padma and *guru-mantra*. At the time of *svarūpa-siddhi* he will understand Gurudeva's position. Śrīla Gurudeva will also arrange *śikṣā-guru* for his disciples to help them achieve *svarūpa-siddhi*. If Guru-pāda-padma doesn't arrange this, then we will go running the wrong way. There is then a big problem.

If there is no attachment with Gurudeva, then we will only have relation with *māyā* and her family. Relatives will tell us, "This is your mother, father, aunt, uncle, brother, sister, grandfather, and grandmother." But Gurudeva gives the identity of our soul and our soul's family.

"Oh! Where are you going?" Gurudeva exclaims, "go to Vṛndāvana, Jagannātha Purī, and Navadvīpa-dhāma. Stay with Vaiṣṇavas, they will protect you. Chant *harināma* there, pray in the morning, hear *hari-kathā* and take *mahā-prasāda*." This is Gurudeva's arrangement and protection. He teaches and helps us, giving us the disposition to gradually progress. This is his causeless mercy. If we forget that Guru-pāda-padma, we will lose everything! And if we always offer obeisance to him with respect, then we will cross *māyā* and enter Vraja.

Raghunātha dāsa Gosvāmī says, "Aho! These senses and family are so attractive. Young age! Wealth! An opulent kingdom! I had everything. This is *mahā-andha-kūpa*, a deep, dark well. How can I escape from this? This is impossible for me. O Gurudeva! You are so kind. You are an ocean of mercy. *He* Gurudeva! On one side my nature pulls me, 'Come, come, there is a nice bed, wife, and all enjoyment! Young age, wealth, everything is available to enjoy.' On the other side you throw your rope of mercy into this well of family life and pull me up, saying, 'Hey! Don't look at this side.' You sent Haridāsa Ṭhākura, Balarāma Ācārya, Advaita Ācārya, and the Gosvāmīs."

Haridāsa Ṭhākura never went near any king. This is not the nature of *sādhus*. It is impossible! He would not go to the homes of wealthy men and beg for any wealth. But he went to the home of the aristocrats Hiranya-Govardhana just to see Raghunātha dāsa Gosvāmī.

When I came to Mathurā, Śrīla Gurudeva taught me, "Never go and beg, 'Oh, give me one *paisa*, one *rupee*.' Only beg for the mercy of Guru and Vaiṣṇavas, the powerful transcendental personalities in Vraja-maṇḍala, and the Gosvāmīs. Pray to them. Don't be greedy for anything mundane." In this world, if Guru and Vaiṣṇavas don't help us, then the illusory energy of the Lord defeats everyone; it smashes us and makes us into *halavā* and chutney. Then people lick, eat and destroy us, and pass us out like stool. If Guru and Vaiṣṇavas protect us, our backbone will be strong, and our health and wealth will be God's property, dedicated only for His service.

Raghunātha dāsa Gosvāmī prays, "How is your mercy? Aho! You took me out of this deep well, and offered me at the lotus feet of Caitanya Mahāprabhu and Svarūpa Dāmodara. I could not understand this at that time. You are not cruel to me, but very kind. Caitanya-candra is the independent Lord. But you prayed for my sake; He then accepted me and always took care of me. He offered me to Svarūpa Dāmodara, who then taught me everything; all this is your mercy."

Dāsa Gosvāmī first offered obeisances to *guru*, then to *śikṣā-guru*, and to Caitanya-candra. This is the proper process. He says, "Without water, a fish suffers and will leave its body in a minute. The soul is inside the body and is always suffering without love and affection. After sometime it leaves the body, but you watered me with *bhakti-rasa*, saving my life, saving my soul. And you took me out of the small well of suffering in family life and brought me to the great ocean of Caitanya Mahāprabhu's unlimited mercy. And He offered me to Svarūpa Dāmodara. Now there is no shortness of anything. How much water is present in a small well? One day this will be dry and short. But the great ocean of Caitanya-candra's mercy will never be finished."

Only Guru-pāda-padma who is *rāgānugā* can give this *anurāga* to his disciples. He is perfectly able to protect and save them.

Ordinary *gurus* have no spiritual power. After sometime the disciples leave their *guru*, and *guru* leaves his disciples, and everyone runs here and there. Why? They have no link, there is no one watering the soul, they have no *rasa*. Thus they are dry and suffer.

Our beloved Śrīla Gurudeva is not like this. He bestows *bhakti-rasa* and gives us life and nourishment so that we can grow and one day attain our *svarūpa-siddhi*. He arranges so that we can obtain this *rasa*. This is the nature of a pure *guru*. Mundane *gurus* give initiation, take some donation, fill their pockets, and then run away, not thinking about the progress of their disciples' souls. Our Guru-varga is not like this. Therefore this line is running on.

Babies don't understand the help and nourishment of their mother's breast milk. Anything the Guru-varga gives to the conditioned souls is like pure nourishing milk, but the ignorant souls have no knowledge of this great mercy. However, when they meet with *śikṣā-guru*, he can teach and make them qualified; then they can understand *guru's* glory.

If we don't hear this *Vilāpa-kusumāñjali*, then how can we understand *guru* and *bhakti*? And those who say, "Don't read, you have no qualification," actually think, "Oh! You are hiding and suffering in deep and dark wells, rotting there in the sewer plants of material life. This is good for you."

Is this called spiritual instruction? No. If anyone is not greedy for this, then how has he come to *guru*? If you have no desire to cross *māyā* and enter the eternal world, then why have you come to this line? Why have you come here? The Guru-varga strongly teaches us. Therefore this book is present, Dāsa Gosvāmī is present, his advice is present, his philosophy and example is present. By following this, spiritual power will come to you; love, faith, and respect will come. Then you will never lose anything. Then you won't think, "I have lost my Gurudeva. My Gurudeva has departed." What is the meaning of departure?

Gurudeva is eternal, God is eternal, and relation with them is eternal. How does this question come to you? Is Gurudeva ash or smoke? Is he dust or anything mundane? No. To understand our Gurudeva's glories we must come near the Gosvāmīs, who will teach us the nature of Gurudeva and how Śrīla Gurudeva is present even now, bestowing his mercy.

Saṁsāra-phukāra kāne nā paṣibe: we will then not hear the talks of ordinary people. Gurudeva will protect us. He makes a protected area for his sincere disciples so that mundane people don't come and torture them with their mundane desires. They will not come and say, "Come, come with me, make relation with me. I will be your lover. You are my friend. Let's go to the park and the movies."

By drinking this *bhakti-rasa*, you will have no more desire or thirst for material life and shall follow *bhakti* very seriously.

Pray everyday with this *Vilāpa-kusumāñjali*. For those who pray, entering eternal life is not hard, but if we don't follow this line, we will waste millions more lives wandering in *māyā*.

2

Fire and Ash

Vairāgya or real renunciation stems from *viśeṣa-anurāga*, or a special form of love. If you have any desire for this *anurāga* then you must take shelter and pray to those personalities who possess that love. This we see in the sixth verse:

vairāgya-yug-bhakti-rasaṁ prayatnair
apāyayan mām anabhīpsum andham
kṛpāmbudhir yaḥ para-duḥkha-duḥkhī
sanātanas taṁ prabhum āśrayāmi
Vilāpa-kusumāñjali 6

I was unwilling to drink the nectar of *bhakti-rasa* flavored with renunciation, but out of his causeless mercy, Sanātana Gosvāmī made me drink, even though I was unwilling. Therefore he is an ocean of mercy. He is compassionate to fallen souls like me; I offer my respectful obeisances unto his lotus feet.

"I had no desire for *vairāgya-yug-bhakti*," Raghunātha dāsa Gosvāmī said, "but Sanātana Gosvāmī is *para-duḥkha-duḥkhī*, sad to see the suffering of others. The conditioned souls have forgotten their own service, misplaced their love, and gone the wrong way. Therefore they are suffering. If one doesn't collect this *bhakti-rasa*, he will always suffer. Therefore what did Sanātana Gosvāmī do? By trick, he gradually gave me this nectar of *bhakti-rasa*. He taught by his own example how to follow *bhakti*."

bhaktiḥ pareśānubhavo viraktir
anyatra caiṣa trika eka-kālaḥ
prapadyamānasya yathāśnataḥ syus
tuṣṭiḥ puṣṭiḥ kṣud-apāyo 'nu-ghāsam
Śrīmad-Bhāgavatam 11.2.42

> With each mouthful of food that a hungry person takes, three effects are simultaneously accomplished: he obtains satisfaction, he is nourished, and his hunger ceases. Similarly, surrendered souls who are engaged in the performance of *bhajana* simultaneously experience three effects: the awakening of *bhakti* which ultimately develops into *prema*, direct manifestation of Bhagavān's beloved form, and detachment from material objects.

On one side, if there is *bhakti*, then automatically *vairāgya*, detachment, arises. If you externally follow the limbs of *bhakti* but *vairāgya* does not awaken, then you should know that you are not really practicing *bhakti*. *Vairāgya* is the process to protect the soul from mundane attraction. This *vairāgya* is necessary. If we come in contact with too many mundane things, we will lose all good desire. If we want to have *anurāga* for *bhakti*, then it is necessary to have a good guardian. Who is that? Raghunātha dāsa Gosvāmī teaches us to take shelter of Sanātana Gosvāmī. He says, "Without my desire, by force he gave me *bhakti-rasa*. He is the ocean of mercy and thought, 'This person has no knowledge; he drinks drain water.' He told me, 'Oh! Please drink one drop of this *bhakti-rasa*, then taste will come. After that, when you are healthy, you will understand this.' He carefully distributed this *bhakti-rasa* to me daily."

In this world people have *bhakti* for mother, father, country, and society. Many people have a desire for help in furthering their interests, and they think that the helpers for this are great. Some say, "In this life I did nothing wrong. Why am I suffering?" But he does not know that his actions are improper. Independently, with his own choice, he does everything, but this is not helpful for himself and for God's pleasure. God gives all facility and chance, but he takes and misuses everything. He thinks it is right, but in truth it is completely wrong and for this he suffers.

Dāsa Gosvāmī continues, "O Caitanya-candra! Caitanya-candra! Caitanya-candra!" How kind is He? If anyone remembers Him, then His followers take him in their lap and stroke with love, "Oh, you like Caitanya-candra? You are trying to follow Caitanya-candra and His movement? Okay, I will help you."

yatheṣṭaṁ re bhrātaḥ! kuru hari-hari-dhvānam aniśaṁ
tato vaḥ saṁsārāmbudhi-taraṇa-dāyo mayi laget
idaṁ bāhu-sphoṭair aṭati raṭayan yaḥ pratigṛhaṁ
bhaje nityānandaṁ bhajana-taru-kandaṁ niravadhi
Nityānandāṣṭakam 5

I perpetually worship Śrī Nityānanda Prabhu, the root of the *kṛṣṇa-bhakti* tree, who approached every doorstep, and with upraised arms exclaimed, "O Brothers! Without inhibition, all of you together continuously chant *harināma*. If you do so, I will take the responsibility to deliver you from the ocean of material existence.

Nityānanda Prabhu says, "If you chant *harināma* even once, then I will run to you! I will maintain you in every way, I will take care of everything. You will be free of all worry."

Raghunātha dāsa Gosvāmī says, "I only heard Caitanya Mahāprabhu's name from my Gurudeva. I heard and remembered Him. I went to Him and Svarūpa Dāmodara always took care of me; all the Vaiṣṇavas took care of me. Without any condition, Sanātana Gosvāmī came to me and took care of me. He taught me the process of *bhakti* and made me drink this *bhakti-rasa*."

aty-utkatena nitarāṁ virahānalena
dandahyamāna-hṛdayā kila kāpi dāsī
hā svāmini kṣaṇam iha praṇayena gāḍham
ākrandhanena vidhurā vilapāmi padyaiḥ
Vilāpa-kusumāñjali 7

O Devī, a certain maidservant, overwhelmed with love and her heart always burning in the great fire of separation, laments in the following verses.

If anyone's nearest and dearest is Śrīla Gurudeva, then Śrīla Gurudeva maintains and takes care of him with his love. What are the symptoms? Aside from Śrīla Gurudeva, he doesn't know anything else. His heart always burns in Śrīla Gurudeva's separation. Day and night he only cries and weeps. He has no desire for anything else.

With deep humility Dāsa Gosvāmī Prabhu prays for eternal service. He says, "I am your insignificant *dāsī*, maidservant. I am very small and low. On the bank of Govardhana I sit in one corner, and cry and pray to You. I cannot take anything by force. I have no good qualities so that You would accept me. I don't follow any good process to enter Vraja-maṇḍala. I don't know anything. Aside from Your causeless mercy I have no hope.

"Now my heart is burning in the fire of separation. My life is finished, I have lost everything. I am unable to serve You. Now I have come to the bank of Girirāja Govardhana, Your nearest and dearest. If I pray to him, he may give me good inspiration. Please accept this prayer and give me some *adhikāra* for Your eternal service."

devi duḥkha-kula-sāgarodare
dūyamānam ati-durgataṁ janam
tvaṁ kṛpā-prabala-naukayādbhutaṁ
prāpaya sva-pada-paṅkajālayam

Vilāpa-kusumāñjali 8

O Devī, please rescue this unfortunate person drowning in an ocean of pain. Place him on the strong boat of Your mercy and carry him to the wonderful realm of Your lotus feet.

He says, "O Rādhe! I am not merely sad, I have fallen in the ocean of distress where I am burning in separation. I don't know how to come out. Be merciful upon me, send a boat to help and carry me across this ocean to Your lotus feet. They are my all and all. Please bring me close to Your lotus feet. Otherwise, for millions of lives I take shelter of ordinary people, but they don't accept me. They only kick me. O Rādhike, You are my life and soul. Please give me shelter. This will be my permanent post and service. Otherwise, I have no power."

Rādhārānī may say, "Oh, why are you sad? Why are you disturbed? Why are you crying?"

"O Devī! Before, I had no knowledge that this world is a prison. Many cruel animals are present who are always cheating me, stealing my life. They appear like friends but they only steal my life, time, and energy. They make me perform bad *karma*, sending me away from *bhakti* and God.

"By the mercy of Caitanya Mahāprabhu and Guru-pāda-padma, I have realized this and come here. Without Your mercy it is not possible to cross over this mundane world. I cannot cross beyond this attachment. If I have no protection and shelter, then I would be forced to go back. If You don't give taste and relation, then I would have to go to others and work constantly for their pleasure.

"I have no shelter. Without You I am very small. Your lotus feet are very wonderful. Many millions and millions of *siddha-sevakas* are present there.

"Please give me a small place there as well. I will sit by Your lotus feet and Your *sevakas* will teach and guide me."

In the ninth verse Dāsa Gosvāmī prays:

tvad-alokana-kalāhi-daṁśair eva mṛtaṁ janam
tvat-padābja-milal-lakṣa-bheṣajair devi jīvaya

Vilāpa-kusumāñjali 9

> O Devī, with the medicine of the red lac from Your lotus feet, please bring back to life this person now dead from the bites of the black snake of not seeing You.

"O Devī, I can't see You. The serpent of time is stealing away my life. It bites me and injects me with poison. I can't protect myself. By its poison I am suffering and feeling so much pain. O Devī! *Tat-padābjam*, Your lotus feet are like life-giving medicine. Please give me life and strength, so that I may return to You. Now I am wounded, as if dead by the influence of *mahā-kāla*. Poisonous snakes always come and bite me. Babies go to their mother and father, who take them in their lap, and kiss and play with them. With all types of love and affection, relatives poison us and keep us disconnected from our soul and the Supreme Soul. These family members are the soldiers of time.

"O Devī, Your lotus feet are covered with reddish *kuṁkum*. Please give me a particle of *kuṁkum* from Your feet. This medicine will cure the material disease and bestow *anurāga*."

Caitanya Mahāprabhu covered Himself with this *anurāga*. In *Anurāga-vallari*, Viśvanātha Cakravartī Ṭhākura wrote that in the early morning Śrīmatī Rādhārānī watched many *pulina-kanyās* going to collect dry wood and cow dung. They saw Kṛṣṇa's foosteps and *kuṁkum* on the grass. Where did this come from? The Vraja-devīs put Kṛṣṇa's feet on their breasts that are smeared with *kuṁkum* and that *kuṁkum* becomes imprinted on the grass when Kṛṣṇa walks through the forest. The *pulina-kanyās* place this *kuṁkum* on their heads and chests. Śrīmatī sees this and says, "How much love they have for this Kṛṣṇa!"

Caitanya-candra wore cloth the reddish color of this *anurāga*. He said, "I always keep the Vraja-devīs' footdust with Me. This footdust is their *anurāga*."

This *anurāga* color is medicine that treats our material condition. How can *hṛd-roga*, lust, go? Dāsa Gosvāmī Prabhu says, "If you take a little bit of this footdust and smear it on your body and pray to that dust, then your *hṛd-roga* will go away. The serpents of time will no longer bite you. Even if you can't bring Her feet directly in your heart, if you can collect a little of this *kuṁkum* and place it in your heart, then that will cure you and bring you to Vraja-dhama."

Some people say, "I have no time, when can I chant? I will chant later. I will serve later." This is the poisonous effect of *kāla-sarpa*, the serpents of time. If you want to be saved from these serpents, then you must take shelter of the Vraja-devis' foot dust.

vande nanda-vraja-strīṇāṁ pāda-reṇum abhīkṣṇaśaḥ
yāsāṁ hari-kathodgīrṇaṁ punāti bhuvana-trayam
Śrīmad-Bhāgavatam 10.47.63

I constantly glorify the dust of the feet of the women of Nanda's cowherd pastures. Their chanting of the activities of Śrī Kṛṣṇa purifies the entire universe.

Brahmā and Uddhava pray like this. This dust is available. Why don't you take it? You don't have the desire. How can desire come? For that desire you must worship Śrīmatī Rādhārāṇī's lotus feet.

Śrīla Narottama dāsa Ṭhākura sings:

rādhikā-caraṇa-renu, bhuṣaṇa koriyā tanu
anāyāse pābe giridhārī
rādhikā-caraṇāśraya, je kore se mahāśaya
tāre moi jāo bolihārī

Ornament your body with the dust of Śrīmatī Rādhikā's lotus feet and you will easily attain Giridhārī. I congratulate such a great soul who takes shelter of Śrīmatī Rādhārāṇī's lotus feet.

jaya jaya rādhā-nāma vṛndāvana jāra dhāma
kṛṣṇa-sukha vilāsera nidhi
heno rādhā guṇa gāna, na sunilo mora kāna
vañcito korilo more vidhi

All glories, all glories to She whose name is Rādhā, whose divine abode is Vṛndāvana, and who is a treasury of pastimes that bring joy to Kṛṣṇa. Alas! If my ears have not heard Rādhā's glories, then destiny has cheated me.

Everything we sing, we sing without desire to accept. We sing, pray, and pass our time, and then run another way. Why? We have no desire to accept this.

Dāsa Gosvāmī Prabhu says, "Color yourself from top to bottom with this *kuṁkum*. Then nothing else can touch or disturb you."

If we don't read the Gosvāmīs' books, like this *Vilāpa-kusumāñjali*, how can we understand what process the Gosvāmīs left for us? How can we cross *māyā*? How can we collect *bhakti-rasa*? Without this, our lives pass uselessly. If we only cry and think about the negative, what benefit will come to us? We accept nothing positive. We will be weak if we take no food and have no *rasa*. *Vaidhī-mārga* is not useless, but who can actually follow all rules and regulations? Those who have *anurāga* follow all rules and regulations naturally. They come everyday to *maṅgala-āratī* to serve in *niśānta-līlā*. There is no need to bang on their doors and shout, "Wake up!" They naturally follow everything with *anurāga*. *Vaidhī-mārga* followers do everything by force. If sometimes they are sick, then how can they follow? This *anurāga* is the only thing necessary for strength in *bhajana*.

devi te caraṇa-padma-dāsikāṁ
viprayoga-bhara-dāva-pāvakaiḥ

dahyamānatara-kāya-ballavīṁ
jīvaya kṣaṇa-nirīkṣaṇāmṛtaiḥ

Vilāpa-kusumāñjali 10

O Devī, with the nectar of a moment's glance, please restore the life of this maidservant of Your lotus feet, who now burns in the great forest-fire of separation from You.

What does Devī mean? In the transcendental realm of Vṛndāvana-dhāma, You control Śrī Kṛṣṇa with Your over-world-power-love and keep Him always near You, thus You are Devī.

"O Devī, I am burning; my body, mind, and senses—everything is burning. Everywhere I look there is only fire, dryness, and ashes. Please cool me with the nectar from Your lotus feet. Śiva Ṭhākura sits in a crematorium and smears his body with ashes, saying, 'In this world there is only fire and ash, fire and ash.' O Devī, this world is a forest-fire and my body is like a burning creeper. I am a very small *dāsī* at Your lotus feet. *Kṛpā kaṭākṣa bhājanam*—please just once grace me with Your merciful glance. If You don't look at me and take care of me, then everyone will come with fire and attack me, saying, 'Hey, don't do this, do what I am telling, follow me.' The government, educators, parents, friends, and the so-called *gurus* and *ācāryas*—everyone in this world smashes us and squeezes out our life. They like to take all our time and life. But they don't say, 'Follow this line of the Gosvāmīs; this is good for you.' "

When a goat or pig is young and healthy, everyone is ready to check, "How much does it weigh? How tasty will it be?" The fire of peoples' desires burns us. People are always ready to attack and digest us.

Dāsa Gosvāmī says, "Kṛṣṇa is transcendental. He is in my heart, but I can't meet with Him because I am surrounded by fire. How can I cross this fire and go to meet with Kṛṣṇa? It is not possible. I am burning in my desire-fire, lust-fire, anger-fire, and so many other fires. I collect fire from all others; they give me this by force. Also, I am sentimental and sensitive—this is one fire. Even worse is the fire of *pratiṣṭhā*, greed for name and fame. O Devī, if these fires aren't vanquished, I will not be able to cross beyond this fearsome world and reach You. I have been burning, burning, burning for millions of lives. Now I have only a little time left. I cannot tolerate this torment any longer. Without Your merciful glance, I will be burnt to ashes and destroyed. Please give me Your *kṛpā-kaṭākṣa-bhājanam*, without which I cannot cross over this fearsome world.

"This body that You gave is always demanding attention and wants me to be its slave. It is a vortex of fire in which I am always burning. I desire to engage my body always as an instrument of Your service. But these fires are burning me and keep me from serving You. In a forest there are many big trees. Sometimes, when wind rubs them against each other, fire is generated. This fire burns the whole forest down. Similarly, mundane people have fire and they steal us away from *bhakti* and *bhajana*. This is like a forest-fire. How can I protect myself from the fires of this world? I don't know. Please help me.

"Your *darśana* is not possible for me. I can't see you, but You can see me. Please give me Your glance of mercy, otherwise I cannot cross over this world and go to You."

svapne 'pi kiṁ sumukhi te caraṇāmbujāta-
rājat-parāga-paṭavāsa-vibhūṣaṇena
śobhāṁ parām atitarām ahahottamāṅaṁ
bibhrad bhaviṣyati kadā mama sārtha-nāma

Vilāpa-kusumāñjali **11**

O beautiful-faced one, when, even in a dream, will I, by decorating my head with the splendid perfumed powder of Your lotus feet, attain the goal of my life?

"O Sumukhi, beautiful-faced one, You are always pleased. You are never disturbed even if I try to disturb You. You know the position of the fallen souls. You know my situation. When will I take the *kuṁkum* from Your lotus feet upon my head? Is this possible even in a dream? Everyday the *sakhīs* and *mañjarīs* place reddish flower pollen on Your lotus feet. Taking this and smearing it on my head, my head will be cool, and good intelligence will come. I will be able to understand Your advice, and good inspiration will come."

Like parents, the Guru-varga teach and take care of their young children, but their children forget and lose everything. After class, people forget everything. They have no brain or power to catch anything. Is the brain damaged? No. There is so much garbage inside; people always collect garbage and put it into their brain. There is no room for anything to come inside. We are interested in science, art, biology, philosophy, economics, civics, mathematics, and especially in how fast our internet connection is. We have knowledge of many material things, but we have no intelligence to remember and realize Rādhārānī's qualities and glories. But if a little of Your *kuṁkum* comes on my head, then it is possible for some good intelligence to come.

Śrīmatī Rādhārānī is supremely blissful. If anyone remembers Her, then he will also become blissful. It is not a dream; this is the truth. *Anurāga* comes from Her lotus feet. When we smear and decorate our head with the dust from Her feet, then our lives will be successful.

amṛtābdhi-rasa-prāyais tava nūpura-siñjitaiḥ
hā kadā mama kalyāṇi bādhiryam apaneṣyate
Vilāpa-kusumāñjali 12

O beautiful one, when will the sound of Your anklebells, sprinkling drops from an ocean of nectar, cure my deafness?

We don't know what is good for our own welfare. We know that tomorrow we may leave the world, die in an accident, or become lame and blind, yet we are very proud. Why? False pride has defeated us.

"O Kalyāṇi, virtuous one, You know what is best for my welfare. I don't know what *bhakti-rasa* is. I am deaf and dumb. *Hari-kathā* of Your glories is always going on, but I am deaf and dumb, I cannot hear or accept anything. When will that day come that I will hear the jingling of Your anklebells as You walk along the pathway to meet Syāma?"

May we have desire for nothing other than hearing the sound of Her anklebells, announcing Her arrival to bestow Her grace upon us.

3

Moonlit Anklebells

To achieve perfection in *rāgānuga-bhakti*, one must make relation with Śrī Guru and *rūpānuga* Vaiṣṇavas, and follow in their footsteps. The *guru-paramparā* distribute this flow of *bhakti-rasa*. Those who are connected to this *bhakti-rasa* will never become restless, hopeless, and run away. But those who don't appreciate *bhakti*, who are attached to sense enjoyment, they will run away out of fear of *rāgānuga-bhakti*.

Śrīmatī Rādhārānī walks with Her anklebells, which jingle as if saying, "Come with us. We will help you. We touch and serve Śrīmatī Rādhārānī's feet and will give you service tendency."

Sometimes we have a good mood and engage in service, but sometime later we become lazy and leave our service. Why is this not permanent? Rādhārānī's anklebells say, "Are you deaf and dumb, can you not hear my call? Come and follow me. Follow Śrīmatī Rādhārānī's footsteps, and then all help will come to you."

The ears are very restless and always try to hear different sounds, but if just once we hear the jingling sound of Śrīmatī Rādhārānī's anklebells, we will lose all desire to hear mundane sounds. That sound bestows supreme auspiciousness.

śaśakabhṛd-abhisāre netra-bhṛṅāñcalābhyāṁ
diśi vidiśi bhayenodghūrṇitābhyāṁ
vanāni kuvalaya-dala-kośāny eva klptāni yābhyāṁ
kim u kila kalanīyo devi tābhyāṁ jano 'yam

Vilāpa-kusumāñjali **13**

O Devī, with the two bumblebees of the corners of Your eyes, which in the moonlit rendezvous anxiously wander over each direction as if the forest were a jungle of blue lotuses, will You glance upon this person?

Śrīmatī Rādhārānī is so effulgent that Her brilliance increases the light of the full moon, making it difficult to move secretly through the forest. Rādhārānī's eyes move restlessly, searching, "Where is that blue lotus? Is He close or far away? Which *kuñja* is He in? Maybe He is hiding close by. Will that blue lotus attack Me on the way?"

Dāsa Gosvāmī says, "Don't worry, we are guarding the pathway. He is far away, waiting anxiously for Your arrival, listening for any sound of Your approach. He is thinking about You and chanting Your *mantra*."

On the dark moon night Śrīmatī Rādhārānī is difficult to see. She dresses completely in black and walks on a hidden path through the forest, staying close to dark Tamāla trees and other plants and creepers on Her way to the *kuñja-kuṭīra*.

Dāsa Gosvāmī says, "My eyes are greedy for Your *darśana*; I am waiting for Your mercy. I am Your insignificant maidservant. Is Your *darśana* possible for me with these eyes?"

Sādhakas engage in *bhajana*. We go to Guru-pāda-padma with a desire for *hari-kathā* and *guru-sevā*, but there are many cheaters and dacoits waiting to pounce on us:

asad-vārtā-veśyā visṛja mati-sarvasva-haraṇīḥ
kathā mukti-vyāghryā na śṛṇu kila sarvātma-gilanīḥ
api tyaktvā lakṣmī-pati-ratim ito vyoma-nayanīm
vraje rādhā-kṛṣṇau sva-rati-maṇi-dau tvaṁ bhaja manaḥ

Manaḥ-śikṣā 4

asac-ceṣṭā-kaṣṭa-prada-vikaṭa-pāśālibhir iha
prakāmaṁ kāmādi-prakaṭa-pathapāti-vyatikaraiḥ
gale baddhvā hanye 'ham iti bakabhid vartmapa-gaṇe
kuru tvaṁ phutkārān avati sa yathā tvāṁ mana itaḥ

Manah-śikṣā 5

Many cheaters and dacoits, internal and external; mundane people and lust, anger, greed, madness are waiting on both sides, not wanting to give us a chance to hear *hari-kathā* and serve. If we are not distracted and go directly towards Śrīmatī Rādhārāṇī, then Kṛṣṇa will help us and will show us the pathway to meet with Śrīmatī Rādhārāṇī. By chanting Rādhārāṇī's holy names Kṛṣṇa will arrange everything to help you progress.

Dāsa Gosvāmī says, "Śrīmatī Rādhārāṇī is Vṛndāvaneśvarī. For a long time I have been waiting to attain Her service. Now I understand that Rūpa Mañjarī has opened a training center in Vṛndāvana. Before, I had no guardian. I had not offered myself, then who would teach me and make me qualified? Who would help me? I did not know, but now I understand. Rūpa Mañjarī will help me. And even though I have no strong desire for service, she will give greed, strength, and *anurāga*."

There are two types of service: by duty and by love. Anything you do by love is accepted. Service performed out of a sense of duty has no sweetness. Sometimes you do it, but carelessly, with a mood of neglect. One house has many servants. The servants come and perform their duty and thereafter run away. There are many tutors ready to teach and many guardians to train us, but they have no love. Therefore the students never learn anything. Why do people come to Gurudeva and Vaiṣṇavas—to learn the process of loving service in Sevā-kuñja, under guidance of the Vraja-devīs.

Dāsa Gosvāmī prays, "O Vṛndāvaneśvarī, I had no idea before about my guardian who would accept me, who would not only tell me my faults, but who would help change my faulty nature and bring me back from the wrong path, who would be kind and very sweet to me, who is helpful for me. In this world everyone looks for faults but cannot give good qualities. But who is very kind, soft, and helpful? Who doesn't neglect, kick, torture, and throw me out? Love has the power to transform, but the process of love is crooked—helping sometimes by neglect, sometimes by acceptance, and sometimes indirectly."

Śrīla Gurudeva has appeared at a distance and from there he is watching, "Who are the real followers of my principles, my rules and regulations? Are they following or not?" Kṛṣṇa is eternal; Gurudeva is eternal. They arrange Vaiṣṇavas to help. They are the abodes of mercy, but we don't realize how kind they are.

Anything we watch with mundane eyes will cheat us. For example, one person is chanting *harinama*, and is internally serving Girirāja Govardhana. His eyes are open and he is sitting in one place, but he is doing *parikramā* of Girirāja Govardhana within. He is praying, singing, doing *abhiśeka*, cooking, offering *bhoga*, decorating the pathway with flowers, and distributing *prasāda*. But ordinary people think that he is only sitting, doing nothing. They tell him, "Hey rascal, go do some work." They tell it to him twenty times but he doesn't answer; he can't even hear this.

If your eyes can't cross *māyā*, then how can you understand the nature of that transcendental realm?

In this Sevā-kuñja, you must not think that there are only monkeys and it is a dirty place where there are some thorn trees. If you have real knowledge, you will pray and wait for service in the eternal Sevā-kuñja. You will pray to the tutors of Sevā-kuñja: Rūpa Mañjarī, Lavanga Mañjarī, Vilāsa Mañjarī, Rati Mañjarī, Rasa Mañjarī, Vinoda Mañjarī... They are helpers, like nurses, knowing how to give treatment and make us strong and healthy. Gradually, they will teach us and help us learn something. Then we won't look towards *māyā*. This is possible when we develop attachment to Rādhārānī's lotus feet. The Vraja-devīs offer pollen, reddish *kuṁkum*, and *alta* everyday on Rādhārānī's feet. The love of their heart is the reddish color of *anurāga*.

yadavadhi mama kañcin mañjarī rūpa-pūrvā
vraja-bhuvi bata netra-dvandva-dīptiṁ cakāra
tadavadhi bata vṛndāraṇya-rājñi prakāmaṁ
caraṇa-kamala-lakṣā-sandidṛkṣā mamābhūt
Vilāpa-kusumāñjali 14

O queen of Vṛndāvana, since Rūpa Mañjarī filled my eyes with light in the land of Vraja, I have yearned to see the red lac decorating Your lotus feet.

If one drop of that *kuṁkum* touches our body, or if we have a desire to see that and we pray for that, then it is possible to attain Her mercy, and to understand who is favorable and helpful. Then we will make a relation with Her group and group leaders. Rays of love will come from Her lotus feet, and with that love we will be able to understand. Otherwise many cheaters come, trying to make relation with us. Many boys and girls come as thieves and cheaters to steal our blood, but don't look at them. We can stop this by becoming one-pointed to Rādhārāṇī's lotus feet and praying to Her.

anayārādhito nūnaṁ
bhagavān harir īśvaraḥ
yan no vihāya govindaḥ
prīto yām anayad rahaḥ
Śrīmad-Bhāgavatam 10.30.28

Śrīmatī Rādhikā has power to attract even the all-attractive Kṛṣṇa, who worships Her, chanting Her *mantra*, only to obtain a little of Her mercy and blessings.

yadā tava sarovaraṁ sarasa-bhṛṅga-saṅghollasat-
saroruha-kulojjvalaṁ madhura-vāri-sampūritam
sphuṭat-sarasijākṣi he nayana yugma-sākṣād-babhau
tadaiva mama lālasājani tavaiva dāsye rase
Vilāpa-kusumāñjali 15

O Devī, whose eyes are as beautiful as two blossoming lotus flowers, when Your lake, filled with sweet water, and splendid with many blossoming lotus flowers and buzzing bees, appeared before my eyes, I at once began to yearn for the nectar of direct service to You.

When the sun rises, lotuses gradually blossom. My heart and soul is in a dark and dirty place, but the light of Śrīla Gurudeva and the Vaiṣṇavas' mercy will open my spiritual eyes.

Dāsa Gosvāmī says, "In the early morning, a bumblebee goes near flowers and sings. The bumblebee Kṛṣṇa goes in the early morning and sings." How does Kṛṣṇa sing? Like Rāmānanda Rāya sings:

kalayati nayanaṁ diśi diśi valitam
paṅkajam iva mṛdu-māruta-calitam

Rādhā's eyes move in all directions like a lotus moving in a gentle breeze.

Kṛṣṇa sings like this. He is a bumblebee, attached to Rādhārānī's glories; this is His only drink. Without singing Her glories He can't be happy.

What does the Guru-varga distribute? Rice, *dal*, medicine, cloth? No! This is only temporary relief. But the soul is not temporary. Without transcendental *rasa* the soul can never attain its own position. It gets one uniform after another, like that of an elephant, horse, camel, or human. The soul cannot attain its permanent *svarūpa* without the help of *sādhus*. To distribute that transcendental *rasa*, Śrīla Gurudeva, the Vaiṣṇavas, and Kṛṣṇa Himself sing the glories of Śrīmatī Rādhārānī. Dāsa Gosvāmī Prabhu prays for this.

In Vraja-maṇḍala, Rūpa Gosvāmī Prabhu is always very busy. People think he is a *sādhu* with no room and work. What does he do day and night?

Like my Guru Mahārāja, *nitya-līlā-praviṣṭa oṁ viṣṇupāda aṣṭottara-śata* Śrī Śrīmad Bhaktidevānta Vāmana Gosvāmī Mahārāja. In his last two years, he practically stopped talking, eating, and sleeping. His *sevaka* requested, "Take some *prasāda*, Guru Mahārāja," but he wouldn't accept. When they requested him again and again, he said, "I am very busy, I have no time to eat anything or talk with you."

"But Guru Mahārāja, what are you doing that keeps you so busy?"

"On one side Ṭhākurāṇī is giving me many instructions, and on the other side my Gurudeva is giving me instructions for service. I have no time to spare. What should I do? I have no time to eat, talk or do anything in this world."

How can people understand the activities and position of *sādhus*? Therefore Dāsa Gosvāmī Prabhu is saying, "I came to Vraja-maṇḍala and met with Rūpa Gosvāmī Prabhu, and saw that he is very busy, day and night, distributing the nectar of Vraja-maṇḍala. How can I accept that? Please teach and help me. Give me power to accept this and take away all desire to accept anything else. May I have greed only to collect this *unnata-ujjvala-rasa*. Having come to Vraja-maṇḍala, may I forget everything else."

4

Cleansing the Spirit

To attain an eternal relation with the *rūpānuga* Guru-varga and *rāgātmika* Vrajavāsīs, we must follow in the footsteps of Raghunātha dāsa Gosvāmī. By this there will be some hope that one day we may attain that relationship.

One person came to the shore of the ocean but was unable to cross. He doesn't know how to cross. The ocean of material existence is very dangerous. We cannot traverse without help. But if we take shelter of a *rūpānuga* Vaiṣṇava, then he will come with a boat and help us easily cross.

pādābjayos tava vinā vara-dāsyam eva
nānyat kadāpi samaye kila devi yāce
sākhyāya te mama namo 'stu namo 'stu nityaṁ
dāsyāya te mama raso 'stu raso 'stu satyam

Vilāpa-kusumāñjali 16

O Devī, I shall never ask You for anything other than direct service to Your lotus feet. I offer my respectful obeisances again and again to the position of Your friends. But I pray always for that sweet position as Your insignificant maidservant.

Dāsa Gosvāmī prays, "O Devī! I am praying for Your service. You have many followers and servants. May they accept me and help me become Your servant. Please give me this boon. Otherwise, without Your desire and instructions, no one will care for or accept me. Then I will be a failure and useless. I pray to You today for Your service. I never want to be directly Your *sakhī* or friend. I only want to be your servant.

I will stay with Your servants and will serve You continuously. This is my only desire.

"Caitanya-candra offered me to the lotus feet of Girirāja Govardhana and to Your lotus feet in the form of *guñjā-mālā*. From that day I became very greedy to attain Your service. Please accept me. Caitanya-candra offered me to You and said, 'You are the servant of Śrīmatī Rādhārāṇī.' Then, for a long time I studied this process and have now finally come to Your lotus feet. Now I am only praying to You for *dāsya*. Please bestow this boon upon me. May I never desire to serve anyone else."

In this world, many people come near Guru, Vaiṣṇavas, and the holy *dhāma*, but they don't pray for *dāsya*. They pray for something material. And then they go and make a relation with ordinary people and follow their footsteps. They become servants of mundane people; the slaves of companies, spouses, children, parents, and so forth. But they don't pray to Rādhārāṇī, "How will I be Your permanent servant?" This prayer is necessary.

maj-janmanaḥ phalam idaṁ madhu-kaiṭabhāre
mat prārthanīya mad-anugraha eṣa eva
tvad bhṛtya-bhṛtya-paricāraka-bhṛtya-bhṛtya
bhṛtyasya-bhṛtyam iti māṁ smara lokanātha

Mukunda-mālā-stotra 25

O Supreme Lord of all, slayer of the demons Madhu and Kaitabha! Please be merciful to me and grant my prayer that You may remember me as a servant of the servant of the servant of the servant of Your servant's servant.

ayi nanda-tanuja kiṅkaraṁ
patitaṁ māṁ viṣame bhavāmbudhau
kṛpayā tava pāda-paṅkaja-
sthita-dhūli-sadṛśaṁ vicintaya

Śikṣāṣṭaka 5

O Nanda-nandana, as a result of my fruitive activities, I have fallen into this fearful ocean of material existence. Please bestow Your mercy upon this eternal servant of Yours. Consider me to be just like a speck of dust at Your lotus feet and always accept me as Your servant.

Dāsa Gosvāmī prays to Rādhārānī, "I don't desire anything else, only the position of Your servant. This is my prayer. Please accept me. If I become Your *sakhī*, I would be very proud and think that I am great. Then I would go the wrong way. Please give me this small post as Your servant. I will do everything You order. When You are coming from Yāvaṭa with Your *sakhīs*, I will decorate the pathway with flowers." Śrīmatī Rādhārānī gives this active mood—anyhow, anywhere You send me, I am ready for service. I will do anything you say.

ati-su-lalita-lakṣāśliṣṭa-saubhāgya-mudrā-
tatibhir adhika-tuṣṭyā cihnitī-kṛtya bāhū
nakha-dalita-haridra-garva-gaurī priyāṁ me
caraṇa-kamala-sevāṁ hā kadā dāsyasi tvam

Vilāpa-kusumāñjali 17

O my mistress, whose fair complexion scratches with its nails the pride of yellow turmeric, when, happily marking my arms with auspicious markings embraced by charming red lac, will You give me the dear service of Your lotus feet?

"O Gaurī, You are golden-limbed. Not only this, Your body is the deity of Kṛṣṇa's heartfelt love. How can I go to Your lotus feet? When will that day come that You will give me an order to smear flower pollen on Your feet. When will that day come? I will decorate Your feet with the signs of barley, sesame, and flowers. Kṛṣṇa's loving eyes will see these and be very happy.

He will wonder, 'Oh, who has decorated Rādhārānī's lotus feet today? This is a very beautiful decoration.' "

Śrīmatī Rādhārānī is the color of molten gold. This, however, is a mundane example, and cannot fully describe Rādhārānī's beauty and effulgence. Gold is hard but Rādhārānī is very soft and sweet. All Kṛṣṇa's love is present with Her, and from there it spreads everywhere in this world to all living entities.

Dāsa Gosvāmī prays, "Please give me some chance for the service of decorating Your feet. Taking *kuṁkum* and saffron pollen full of *anurāga*, I will decorate Your feet."

Then he feels, "I will serve Her feet for some time, but if I am separate, then I will not always be there at Her feet." So he then prays, "How can I be like one particle of *kuṁkum* on Your lotus feet, always serving You. I desire to remain always at Your feet. O Rādhike, when will that day come that, in the early morning, I will wash Your feet and then smear a mixture of sandalwood paste, saffron, *mehindi*, and *gorocanā* on them?

"As you walk from Yāvaṭa to Nandagāon to cook in the kitchen for Kṛṣṇa, I will clean the kitchen, bring pots and utensils, and arrange everything. When will that day come that You give me a chance to serve?"

Dāsa Gosvāmī is factually present in his soul's *svarūpa* as Rati Mañjari with Śrīmatī Rādhārānī. He prays like this to give us an indication and greed to attain the service of Rādhārānī.

praṇālīṁ kīlālair bahubhir abhi saṅkṣalya madhurair
mudā sammarjya svair vivṛta-kaca-vṛndaiḥ priyatayā
kadā bāhyāgāraṁ vara-parimalair dhūpa-nivahair
vidhāsye te devi pratidinam aho vāsitam aham

Vilāpa-kusumāñjali 18

O Devī, when, with great love and happiness, will I daily rinse the drains of Your house with pure water, dry them with my own hair, and then scent Your garden pavilion with an abundance of sweetly fragrant incense?

Dāsa Gosvāmī prays, "Everyday, with clean water, I will wash all the drains nearby Nanda-bhavana."

Many impure things are in our hearts. The Guru-varga carefully perform *ceto-darpaṇa-mārjanam*; they clean our hearts, which are now filthy, like a drain. The Guru-varga clean our *anarthas* and Vaiṣṇavas take a broom and sweep and wash our hearts. They do this very carefully, not roughly, with a soft brush, broom, and cloth.

Dāsa Gosvāmī says, "The drain is my good friend. I will daily clean the drains in Nandagrāma, Varsānā, and Yāvaṭa. Then I will place perfumes, scents, and incense inside them. When will that glorious day come?" He is crying and his tears are flowing. This is the process of prayer. First Dāsa Gosvāmī prays for the service of Rādhārānī's lotus feet. Then he says, "This is not enough for me. My Śrīmatī Rādhārānī walks on this path. If I don't clean it, then how can I feel well?" A temple doesn't mean only the *pūjārī's* room or the Deity's room. The temple area includes the garden, drain, kitchen, *brahmacārīs'* rooms and so forth. If everything is dirty, then that is not God's place; then it is not a temple, it is a *tāmasika* place for ghosts and spirits. A temple should always be clean, then *nirguṇa* Hari will preside there.

Wherever Śrīmatī Rādhārānī goes, the *mañjaris* make everything fragrant. Narottama dāsa Ṭhākura, Śyāmānanda, and Śrīnivāsa came to Śrīla Jīva Gosvāmī to learn from him. One day, Śyāmānanda Prabhu asked Jīva Gosvāmī, "You have taught us the books of the Gosvāmīs, now, how can practical realization of these subjects come to us?"

"You must practice what you have been taught through service," Śrīla Jīva Gosvāmī said. "Go and sweep the pathways of Vṛndāvana."

But now we only talk and theorize, and if we are told to take a broom and sweep, after a few minutes we say, "My back hurts. I am a high-class person, how can I do such a demeaning service?"

Prabhodānanda Sarasvatīpada prayed:

yat-kiṅkarīṣu bahuśaḥ khalu kāku-vāṇī,
nityaṁ parasya puruṣasya śikhaṇḍa-mauleḥ
tasyāḥ kadā rasa-nidheḥ vṛṣabhānu-jāyās
tat-keli-kuñja-bhavanāṅgana-mārjanī syām

Rādhā-rasa-sudhā-nidhi 8

O daughter of Vṛṣabhānu Mahārāja, ocean of *rasa*, that beautiful boy who wears a gracefully tilting peacock feather in His hair is actually the original Personality of Godhead. Still, He is always falling at the feet of Your maidservants and pitifully begging them with many humble words to gain entrance into Your *kuñja*, where the two of You engage in Your playful loving pastimes. My life would be successful if I could even be one stick in the broom Your maidservants use to clean Your delightful *kuñja*.

Our Guru-varga pray like this. But now we stay in Vṛndāvana and don't serve Vṛndāvana at all, thinking, "This is cow dung, I can't touch it! It smells so bad!" Or, "How can I clean the kitchen? My body will get dirty." Because we have dirt within, we see only dirt without. Our hearts are dirty, therefore we don't like to clean anything. But even a dog cleans where he sleeps with his tail.

Dāsa Gosvāmī prays, "With my hair I will clean the drains and decorate the pathways of Vraja. When Śrīmatī Rādhārāṇī walks along with the *sakhīs* and *mañjarīs*, She will be pleased that the area is clean and fragrant."

If you desire eternal service, then *svarūpa-śakti* will give you all types of power, potency, taste—everything. Otherwise when serving, the heart becomes dry like a desert. Anywhere we go, we will burn and suffer, because we have no desire to serve. Only theory is not enough. This is knowledge, but how will knowledge become active? We must practically become engaged in some service. Our Guru-varga show us by their example.

Dāsa Gosvāmī prays to clean the drains of Nanda-bhavana and dry them with his hair, but we see that he doesn't have hair in his form as a *sādhaka*. Where does this hair come from?

> *sevā sādhaka-rūpeṇa siddha-rūpeṇa cātra hi*
> *tad-bhāva-lipsunā kāryā vraja-lokānusārataḥ*
>
> *Bhakti-rasāmṛta-sindhu* 1.2.294

> He who has developed greed for *rāgātmikā-bhakti* should closely follow in the footsteps of the particular associates in Vraja whose moods he aspires for. Under their guidance, he should engage in service both in his external form as a *sādhaka*, and internally with his perfected spiritual body.

If we desire *svarūpa-siddhi*, we must serve in the form of a *sādhaka* as well as in our internally contemplated form as Rādhārāṇī's maidservant, and we must be grave and practice strong *vairāgya*. Externally, the bona fide *sādhaka* follows all rules and regulations of *bhakti*, while within he meditates on his service in his *siddha-svarūpa*.

> *prātaḥ sudhāṁśu-militāṁ mṛdam atra yatnād*
> *āhṛtya vāsita-payaś ca gṛhāntare ca*
> *pādāmbuje bata kadā jala-dhārayā te*
> *prakṣālya bhāvini kacair iha mārjayāmi*
>
> *Vilāpa-kusumāñjali* 19

> When, at Your house early in the morning, will I carefully wash Your two lotus feet with camphor-scented water, and then dry them with my hair?

Dāsa Gosvāmī now prays, "When You wake and come out of Your room, I will wash Your feet and dry them with my hair."

At night, the *mañjaris* place sweet, pure water in a clay pot and put a cotton cloth on top of it. They then put some camphor and flowers on the cloth and cover them. The next morning they use this water that is embued with a wonderful fragrance.

Dāsa Gosvāmī says, "Many *ṛṣis*, *maharṣis*, and others are waiting to drink this *caraṇāmṛta*, but without Your permission I will not give one drop to anyone."

When Caitanya Mahāprabhu went to Jagannātha's temple in Purī, He would first wash His feet. But He had Govinda Prabhu wait with Svarūpa Dāmodara to prevent anyone from touching or drinking this water.

But now people consider themselves *mahā-bhāgavatas* able to do anything without any reaction. They put their feet forward and say, "Wash my feet and take the *caraṇāmṛta*, then your life will be successful."

This is not the culture of our *paramparā*. Śrīmatī Rādhārāṇī is very serious and strong, She will not give a drop of the water that washed Her feet to anyone unqualified.

Caitanya Mahāprabhu only gave to one person, Jhaḍū Ṭhākura.

I have heard that some people say on Facebook that there are no real Vaiṣṇavas in our *saṅga*. How do they have this idea? If Jhaḍū Ṭhākura heard that anywhere, anyone was doing *nāma-saṅkīrtana*, he would go and give him a gift of fruit or some *prasāda* and after they ate would anyhow take his remnants. Jhaḍū Ṭhākura would eat the remnants of Vaiṣṇavas and thus made his body sanctified and received the mercy of Mahāprabhu. He went to Jagannātha Purī in his old age and took a handful of Mahāprabhu's footbath water as Mahāprabhu entered the Jagannātha temple, and all the *bhaktas* present there were very surprised to see Mahāprabhu allow this.

Mahāprabhu said, "I know you. You faithfully take the *mahā-prasāda* of all Vaiṣṇavas."

If you don't think there are any Vaiṣṇavas, it means you don't take the *mahā-prasāda* remnants of any Vaiṣṇavas. You eat contaminated *māyā-prasāda*, and this has spoiled your intelligence. You are now blind and can't see any Vaiṣṇavas. Without Vaiṣṇavas, how can *bhakti* run on in this world? How can God be pleased and happy? This world will be destroyed without any Vaiṣṇavas.

prakṣālya pāda-kamalaṁ kṛta-danta-kāṣṭāṁ
snānārtham anya-sadane bhavatīṁ niviṣṭām
abhyājya-gandhitatarair iha taila-pūraiḥ
prodvartayiṣyati kadā kim u kiṅkarīyam
Vilāpa-kusumāñjali 20

When will this maidservant brush Your teeth with a twig, wash Your lotus feet, and, when You have entered another room, massage You with scented oil?

"O Rādhe," Dāsa Gosvāmī prays, "when will that day come that I will wash your feet, smear *arbaṭa, kuṁkum, mehendi,* and *candana* on them, and offer some flowers at Your feet. Then I will arrange for Your bath. First I will massage Your body with oil, and then I will arrange warm water for Your bath. I will give You a toothbrush. Then, I will also massage You with *arbaṭa.*"

Arbaṭa is a mixture of pasted neem, raw turmeric, and mustard seeds. If you go to temples, you will see that in the early morning, after *maṅgala-ārati*, the *pujārīs* smear oils on the Deities, like sesame oil or coconut oil mixed with camphor, and then they apply *arbata*, *candana*, and *kuṁkum* on the Deities. They then bath the Deities and afterwards draw designs on Them with *alta*. By this process, one makes a relation with the Lord. But it is not possible for everyone. One or two *pujārīs* are in a temple doing *puja*, but how can all the other devotees do this? Therefore they should do *mānasi-pūja* everyday. How can devotees establish a relationship with *guru* and Bhagavān? Therefore during *guru-mantra*, they should worship and serve Gurudeva. At the time of chanting *gaura-mantra*, Gaurahari should be internally worshiped, and during *kṛṣṇa-mantra*, Kṛṣṇa should be worshiped. This is called real chanting. We shouldn't just quickly chant mindlessly and then run off. Then we will never make a relation with Kṛṣṇa and His associates. *Mantras* free the mind—*manah trāyate iti mantra*—but we must chant properly. While chanting our *mantras*, we should throw out all the dirt and garbage from our minds and engage them in serving the presiding Deities of the *mantra*. This is the process to follow when chanting our *mantras*. Then the *mantra* liberates the mind. Practice this, and then you will be able to cross *māyā* and get a relation with the eternal world and the Vrajavāsīs.

5

Loving Service of Love Divine

Dāsa Gosvāmī now prays to Rādhāranī:

ayi vimala-jalānāṁ gandha-karpūra-puṣpair
jita-vidhu-mukha-padme vāsitānāṁ ghaṭaughaiḥ
praṇaya-lalita-sakhyā dīyamānaiḥ purastāt
tava varam abhiṣekaṁ hā kadāhaṁ kariṣye
Vilāpa-kusumāñjali 21

O Devī, whose lotus face defeats the moon, when, with jars of water, scented with flowers and camphor, and brought by one of Your charming and affectionate friends, will I carefully bathe You?

The *sakhīs* make many arrangements for the service of Śrīmatī Rādhārānī. Their hearts are like camphor, the essence of fragrant flowers, and pure water. They arrange everything with their heartfelt affection. First they massage Śrīmatī Rādhārānī's body, and then they bathe Her with their love in the form of a bath. When the full moon rises, its rays cool all beings. But the love of the *sakhīs* and *mañjarīs* is millions of times more nectarful and sweet than moonrays. With unparalleled love they perform the *abhiṣeka* of Śrīmatī Rādhārānī. Each *gopī's* love is unique. Yamunā, Gaṅgā, Kāveri—the waters of all the holy rivers have different tastes, colors, and qualities. In the same way, at the time of *abhiṣeka*, the *mañjarīs* and *sakhīs* each come forth with their personal heartfelt love and *rasa* and bathe Śrīmatī Rādhārānī.

Dāsa Gosvāmī prays, "When will that day come when I will offer my heart for Rādhārānī's service?"

pānīyaṁ cīna-vastraiḥ śaśimukhi śanakai
ramya-mṛdv-aṅga-yaṣṭair
yatnād utsārya modād diśi diśi
vicalan-netra-mīnāñcalāyāḥ
śroṇau raktaṁ dukūlaṁ tad aparam atulaṁ
cāru-nīlaṁ śiro 'grāt
sarvāṅgeṣu pramodāt pulakita-vapuṣā
kiṁ mayā te prayojyam

Vilāpa-kusumāñjali 22

O moon-faced one, with a silken towel will I be allowed to slowly and carefully dry the water from Your beautiful, delicate limbs, as the two fishes of Your eyes happily and restlessly swim from one direction to another? The hairs of my body standing up in bliss, will I be allowed to cover Your hips with a matchless red silk cloth, and all Your limbs, from Your head down, with a beautiful blue *sari*?

Many flowers bloom at night and there are many medicinal herbs that receive nectar from the moon. The moon distributes nectar. At the time of Śrīmatī Rādhārānī's *abhiṣeka*, many *sakhīs* and *mañjarīs* bathe Her with their eyes and perform Her *ārati*. Then, like the moon, Śrīmatī Rādhārānī nourishes all the *sakhīs* and *mañjarīs* with Her merciful glance.

Śrīmatī Rādhārānī's body is very soft, and She is wearing a thin silken cloth. The *sakhīs* and *mañjarīs* remove this cloth and bathe Her, and then dress Her with a new silken cloth. Dāsa Gosvāmī prays, "When will that day come when I arrange for Her bath? After Her *abhiṣeka*, I will dry Her Divine Form with a soft, scented towel, and will then decorate Her with my own hands.

"O Rādhike, the water on Your body does not want to leave You. It came to serve You—to cool You and wash Your body. Many drops remain on Your body like pearls, not willing

to ever leave You. I wish to dry Your body, but the drops of water wish to stay with You forever. I will dry Your form very carefully. Then, I will cover Your head with a blue cloth and decorate You with *tilaka* and *alaka*. Please instruct me at that time. I will follow those instructions very carefully."

prakṣālya pāda-kamalaṁ tad-anukrameṇa
goṣṭhendra-sūnu-dayite tava keśa-pāśam
hā narmadā-grathita-sundara-sūkṣma-mālyair
veṇīṁ kariṣyati kadā praṇayair jano 'yam

Vilāpa-kusumāñjali 23

O beloved of the prince of Vraja, when, after washing Your lotus feet, will this person, with the many beautiful small garlands, artistically fashioned by Narmadā-devī, lovingly braid Your hair?

"O Rādhe, You are the dearest beloved of the son of Nanda Mahārāja. I am waiting for Your service. When will I save the water that bathes Your lotus feet? I will save this, like Your *svarūpa*, near me. As the water served You, it will always give me desire and inspiration and will make my heart melt."

Brahmā collected the footwash water of the Lord in his *kamaṇḍalu* pot. He kept that with him and offered *praṇāma* to it. He used to drink it and was very pleased. In the same way, the *caraṇāmṛta* of Rādhārāṇī is transcendental.

Raghunātha dāsa Gosvāmī says, "I will comb Your hair and decorate it with delicate, white flowers. O beloved of Nanda-nandana! Having bathed and dressed You in fresh cloth, I will wash Your feet. I will apply *candana, aguru,* and *kastūrī* to Your lotus feet, and will decorate them with *alaka*. I will first bathe Your feet with camphor water. I will then dry Your feet and cover them with sandalwood paste. I will then wash off the sandal with *kastūrī* and *gorocana* water. Then I will bathe

Your feet with *pañcāmṛta*—cow milk, yogurt, honey, ghee, and sugar. Thereafter, I will wash Your feet with pure water and smear flower pollen on them."

subhaga-mṛgamadenākhaṇḍa-śubhrāṁśu-vat te
tilakam iha lalāṭe devi modād vidhāya
masṛṇa-ghusṛṇa-carcām arpayitvā ca gātre
stana-yugam api gandhaiś citritaṁ kiṁ kariṣye

Vilāpa-kusumāñjali 24

O Devī, when will I happily place on Your forehead beautiful musk *tilaka* as splendid as the full moon, on Your limbs glistening *kuṁkum*, and on Your chest wonderful pictures in fragrant colors?

Dāsa Gosvāmī next prays, "When I will decorate Your forehead with cooling *kastūrī-tilaka*? When will anoint Your hands and chest with *kuṁkum*, *candana*, and *āguru*. I will decorate Your cheeks with pleasing designs.

sindūra-rekhā sīmānte devi ratna-śalākayā
mayā yā kalpitā kiṁ tesālakaṁ śobhayiṣyati

Vilāpa-kusumāñjali 25

O Devī, when will I, drawing a line of red *sindūra* with a jeweled *śalākā*, decorate the part in Your hair?

"O Rādhe, when will I place red *sindūra* in the part of Your hair with a golden stick. Later, by Your order, I will take this and smear it on Kṛṣṇa's feet. I will always be ready for this service."

hanta devi tilakasya samastād
bindavo 'ruṇa-su-gandhi-rasena
kṛṣṇa-mādaka-mahauṣadhi-mukhyā
dhiṛa-hastam iha kiṁ para-kalpyāḥ

Vilāpa-kusumāñjali 26

O Devī, when, with a steady hand, will I artistically decorate You with the aromatic red *tilaka* dots that are the most powerful aphrodisiac to madden Kṛṣṇa?

Dāsa Gosvāmī prays, "O Devī, when will I decorate Your face with the medicinal nectar of flowers. By seeing this, Kṛṣṇa's burning heart will be cooled."

The *gopīs* collect the juice of many flowers with their heartfelt love. Their love shines in each and every drop of *alaka* decorating Śrīmatī Rādhārāṇī's face. The color is like the reddish color of the rising and setting sun. This is the color of *anurāga* and decorates the head of Śrīmatī Rādhārāṇī. Like the Sun who rides a chariot drawn by many brilliant horses, Śrīmatī Rādhārāṇī's body is adorned with *alaka*.

Some times, when Śrīmatī Rādhārāṇī is anguished in separation from Kṛṣṇa, if by chance She looks at Her own face in a mirror or in water, the image of Kṛṣṇa, performing pastimes wherever He may be at that moment, reflects in Her *alaka* decorations. When Rādhārāṇī is sad, the *sakhīs* show Her reflection in a mirror and say, "Look at Kṛṣṇa. He is also thinking of You. He will come very soon." This is the best medicine. When Kṛṣṇa looks at Rādhārāṇī's *alaka*, He can understand Her moods.

goṣṭhendra-putra-mada-citta-karīndra-rāja-
bandhāya puṣpa-dhanuṣaḥ kila bandha-rajjoḥ
kiṁ karṇayos tava varoru varāvataṁsa-
yugmena bhūṣaṇam ahaṁ sukhitā kariṣye

Vilāpa-kusumāñjali 27

O beautiful one, when will I happily decorate Your ears with beautiful earrings, which are cupid's two ropes for binding the heart of the regal mad elephant, the Prince of Vraja?

"O beautiful-thighed one, You have the greatest ability to serve Kṛṣṇa. You know how to please Him. Nanda-nandana is very proud, like an elephant cub moving carelessly in a garden. No one can catch or control Him. Great *ṛṣis* and *maharṣis* have no power to catch Him. Even Yaśodā Mātā tried again and again, but could only bind Him to the grinding mortar by His own mercy. To bind Kṛṣṇa and keep Him close—no one has this power. Only You have this ability."

Beautiful earrings adorn Kṛṣṇa's ears. Śrīmatī Rādhārāṇī has a sweet relationship with those earrings. His earrings hear Her speech and they swing and tell Kṛṣṇa, "These words just came to us. Now hear them." As the earrings sway to and fro, they touch Kṛṣṇa's cheeks and say, "Wait. Stop running. We will peacefully tell You all the news sent by Rādhārāṇī."

Dāsa Gosvāmī says, "I will also give earrings to Rādhārāṇī. Like dear friends, they will receive and deliver to Śrīmatī Rādhārāṇī the messages sent by Kṛṣṇa."

In the heavenly planets, Indra is the king. But in Vraja-maṇḍala, Kṛṣṇa is not merely the king. He has full sovereignty over everyone's heart. He has won the hearts of all the Vrajavāsīs. Therefore He is Goṣṭhendra. The Vrajavāsīs never take Him from their hearts. They all desire that He forever remain in their hearts. However, Kṛṣṇa is controlled by Śrīmatī Rādhārāṇī. She arranges many special ornaments for Kṛṣṇa. Her *sakhīs* and *mañjarīs* give new earrings to Kṛṣṇa everyday, made of flowers and jewels. The *mañjarīs* also daily give Śrīmatī Rādhārāṇī new earrings. To control the elephant cub Kṛṣṇa, these earrings are required. These earrings are the remedy for His arrogance.

6

A Holy Attempt

In the early morning, the Vraja-devīs pick flowers with heartfelt love. They pick flowers that are soft, aromatic, full of nectar, and newly blossomed. They take the flowers and put their love and affection inside each one. "Dear flowers," they say, "we cannot go where you are going. You are going to embrace Kṛṣṇa's charming neck. You will rest on His chest and will embrace and kiss Him. All this is not possible for us. You are not merely flowers, you are our representatives."

When the Vraja-devīs choose flowers to be offered to Kṛṣṇa's lotus feet, they worry, "Will Kṛṣṇa accept these from us or not?" Therefore, they first offer them to Rādhārāṇī. The flowers transfer the love of the *gopīs* to Śrīmatī Rādhārāṇī and then to Kṛṣṇa. When they are touched by Śrīmatī Rādhārāṇī, the flowers are infused with more energy. Then they become powerful enough to bind and arrest Kṛṣṇa. Sometimes they are used in His garland, sometimes they touch His feet, and sometimes their fragrant pollen is used for His *abhiṣeka*. While kissing Him again and again, the flowers deliver the message of the *gopīs*.

yā te kañculir atra sundari mayā
vakṣojayor arpitā
śyāmācchādana-kāmyayā kila na sā
tathyeti vijñāyatām
kintu svāmini kṛṣṇa eva sahasā
tat tām avāpya svayaṁ
prāṇebhyo 'py adhikaṁ svakaṁ
nidhi-yugaṁ saṅgopayaty eva hi

Vilāpa-kusumāñjali 28

> O beautiful Devī, although I carefully placed this garment over Your chest to cover it from Kṛṣṇa's gaze, He has not understood my intention. Tightly embracing You, He has Himself become the garment covering Your chest, dearer than His own life.

Dāsa Gosvāmī says, "O embodiment of beauty, sometimes You wear a blue dress, sometimes a black dress, or a rose-colored dress, and You hide Yourself from Śyāma. You cover Your face and body with cloth and hide from Kṛṣṇa. But Kṛṣṇa comes from a hidden direction and tries to embrace You.

"You hide in a secret place, not wanting to give Him *darśana*, but He is very greedy to see You. He asks Your nearest and dearest *mañjarīs*, 'Where is your Svāminī? How can I see Her? I am very thirsty for Her *darśana*. I must have Her *darśana*.'"

Śrīmatī Rādhārāṇī is close, but Her face and body are covered by cloth that matches the scenery around Her, and Kṛṣṇa cannot see Her. The color of Her cloth enables Her to blend into the leaves and flowers in the *kuñja*. She is sitting with the *mañjarīs*, and Kṛṣṇa is unaware of Her presence, but He is maddened by Her fragrance. Śrīmatī watches in amusement as Kṛṣṇa pleads with the *mañjarīs* for Her *darśana*.

Dāsa Gosvāmī continues, "At the time of dressing You, I will adorn Your limbs with a wonderful cloth. I will carefully place that cloth on You so that Śyāma cannot remove it, but He is waiting for Your *darśana*, and sometimes He enters the *kuñja* by force."

Dāsa Gosvāmī is in the body of a man in his *sādhaka* form. How can he have this mood of dressing Rādhārāṇī? How can he bathe Her or massage Her Divine Form? This is his *Vilāpa-kusumāñjali*. He is present there in his form as a *mañjari* and is eternally engaged in this sweet, intimate service. He has bestowed these prayers for *sādhakas* to develop their greed for entrance into eternal Vraja. By remembering the pastimes of that *sac-cid-ānanda-vigraha*, the mind, heart, and desires will automatically be purified.

ānanda-cinmaya-rasa-pratibhāvitābhis
tābhir ya eva nija-rūpatayā kalābhiḥ
goloka eva nivasaty akhilātma-bhūto
govindam ādi-puruṣaṁ tam ahaṁ bhajāmi
Brahma-saṁhitā 5.37

Govinda, who is all-pervading and who exists within the hearts of everyone, resides in His Goloka-dhāma along with Rādhikā, who is the embodiment of His pleasure potency and the counterpart of His own spiritual form. She is the epitome of transcendental *rasa*, and is expert in the sixty-four arts. They are also accompanied by the *sakhīs*, who are expansions of Rādhikā's own transcendental body, and who are infused with blissful, spiritual *rasa*. I worship that original personality, Śrī Govinda.

Real *sannyāsa* is possible when this transcendental *rasa* enters within you and makes you qualified. Then strong *vairāgya* develops and you will have no relation or attachment to anything in this world. Such a *sannyāsī* can enter Vraja-maṇḍala for the eternal service of Rādhā and Kṛṣṇa. If you have not taken this *sannyāsa*, you cannot enter that world.

nānā-maṇi-prakara gumphita-cāru-puṣṭyā
muktā-srajas tava su-vakṣasi hema-gauri
śrānty-abhṛtālasa-mukunda-su-tūlikāyāṁ
kiṁ kalpayiṣyatitaraṁ tava dāsikeyam
Vilāpa-kusumāñjali 29

O golden-complexioned one, when will this maidservant place lovely necklaces of pearls and jewels on Your chest, the resting place of Mukunda?

Dāsa Gosvāmī prays, "O golden Rādhe! I am your insignificant *dāsī*. When will I decorate Your chest, the resting place of Mukunda, with jeweled necklaces?"

The ornaments made by the servants of Śrīmatī Rādhārāṇī have special powers. They steal away fatigue from their wearer and give new strength. Śrīmatī Rādhārāṇī's body is like molten gold. She already has everything. She is *svarūpa-śakti*, the Divine Potency Herself. She is never tired, weak, or needing any help. What help can She be given? But She accepts these loving gifts of Her maidservants. Then these ornaments become even more powerful. When they are next offered to Kṛṣṇa, He is overwhelmed with bliss. Śrīmatī Rādhārāṇī gives *adhikāra* for this service.

maṇi-caya-khacitābhir nīla-cūḍāvalībhir
hari-dayita-kalāvid-dvandvam indīvarākṣi
api bata tava divyair aṅgulīr aṅgulīyaiḥ
kvacid api kila kāle bhūṣayiṣyāmi kiṁ nu

Vilāpa-kusumāñjali 30

O lotus-eyed one, when will I adorn Your fingers with glittering rings, and Your two graceful arms, which are so dear to Hari, with blue armlets studded with jewels?

Dāsa Gosvāmī prays, "When will I place jewel-studded rings on Your fingers and blue armlets on Your arms?"

On Kṛṣṇa's hands there are wonderful rings. The *sakhīs* and *mañjarīs* remove these rings from His fingers and clean them. Why do they take them? Everyday, with His own hand, Kṛṣṇa applies *kuṁkum* and *alaka* on the lotus feet and body of Śrīmatī Rādhārāṇī. Sometimes He makes a beautiful crown and offers it to Śrīmatī Rādhārāṇī. Sometimes He wears Rādhārāṇī's rings and gives His *cūḍāmaṇi* and *kaustubha-maṇi* to Her. But before He leaves to go home, the *sakhīs* exchange the ornaments again. Why? When Kṛṣṇa goes back to Nanda-bhavana, if He was wearing Rādhārāṇī's ornaments, everyone would tease Him. Therefore the *sakhīs* take Kṛṣṇa's ornaments from Rādhārāṇī's hands and come running to Kṛṣṇa to give them back. Kṛṣṇa's eyes are tinged with red on the sides. The *sakhīs* watch His eyes and make a crown. Their hands have bangles. With these bangles they make a crown. When Kṛṣṇa touches His crown, He understands which piece is from which *sakhī* and *mañjarī*. The *sakhīs* and *mañjarīs* give Kṛṣṇa some rings that are very dear to them. Kṛṣṇa wears these rings for some time and then gives them back. Sometimes the *gopīs* give Kṛṣṇa bangles with designs made of many minerals.

When the *sakhās* see Kṛṣṇa, they are surprised and say, "Why are You wearing bangles today?"

"I am just a small boy now," Kṛṣṇa replies. "Soon I will be a young man and much bigger and healthier. Now this looks like a bangle, but when I grow up it will be My ring. My hand is small now. So I wear this as a bangle only for now, but when I grow up, it will be My ring."

Kṛṣṇa jokes with the *sakhās* in ways like this. The *gopīs* watch and laugh with Śrīmatī Rādhārāṇī from a distance.

pādāmbhoje maṇimaya-tulā-koṭi-yugmena yatnād
abhyarcyaitad-dala-kulam api prestha-pādāṅgulīyaiḥ
kāñcī-dāmnā kaṭi-taṭam idaṁ prema-pīṭhaṁ su-netre
kaṁsārāter atulam acirād arcayiṣyāmi kiṁ te

Vilāpa-kusumāñjali 31

O beautiful-eyed one, when will I worship Your two lotus feet with jeweled anklets and the petals of Your lotus feet with toe-rings? With a splendid belt, when will I worship Your hips, the sacred pilgrimage place of Kaṁsārī?

Dāsa Gosvāmī prays, "When will I place anklets and toe-rings on Your lotus feet? Then I will take a soft cotton brush and paint designs on those shining ornaments, using ink made from flowers of different colors. Sometimes I will paint lotus petals, sometimes roses, jasmines, or other flowers on Your feet. Every day I will arrange newer and newer kinds of anklebells. They will be bedecked with jewels and minerals and with small fragrant flowers."

Kṛṣṇa attracts everyone, but Raghunātha dāsa Gosvāmī knows who attracts Him. He says, "After fastening flower anklebells and anklets upon them, I will make artistic decorations on those two feet. Kṛṣṇa will come from a distance and say, 'Who is this Goddess?' He will then come forward and offer *puṣpāñjali* at Your lotus feet. This is my desire. These feet are respected all over the three worlds. They are the storehouse of limitless blessings and mercy. O Rādhike, I will first do *arcana* of Your feet in this way."

Dāsa Gosvāmī next prays:

lalitatara-mṛṇāli-kalpa-bāhu-dvayaṁ te
murajayi-mati-haṁsī-dhairya-vidhvaṁsa-dakṣam
maṇi-kula-racitābhyām aṅgadābhyāṁ purastāt
pramada-bhara-vinamrā kalpayiṣyāmi kiṁ vā

Vilāpa-kusumāñjali 32

Bowed down with intense bliss, when will I decorate Your two graceful arms with jeweled armlets, which expertly destroy the peacefulness of the swan of Kṛṣṇa's heart?

"O Rādhike! Murāri's mind is restless and uncontrolled. He has no patience or tolerance. He is always greedy for Your *darśana* and embrace. After decorating Your body in various ways, I will place You on a regal seat so that Kṛṣṇa may have *darśana* of You from afar. Kṛṣṇa is very greedy. He cannot control Himself. Rather, He runs toward You for an embrace, thinking, 'Oh! *Darśana* of this Goddess is not enough. I must go nearby Her to collect Her blessings.' Then He prays to You with many verses. These verses spring from Kṛṣṇa's heart like lotus stems, rising up from below the surface of an autumn lake. The lotus comes up and shows, "I have such sweet nectar, fragrance, and color."

Because Kṛṣṇa killed the demon named Mura, He is called Murāri. He is very strong and powerful. But in front of Rādhikā, He has no self-control. He tries to fly to Rādhārāṇī like a swan, eager to eat a lotus stem. He wants to embrace Her, but the *mañjarīs* give Him no such chance. After Her *abhiṣeka* and decoration, Rādhārāṇī sits and plays with Her *sakhīs* in a secluded grove, guarded by the *mañjarīs*.

rāsotsave ya iha gokulacandra-bāhu-
sparṣeṇa saubhaga-bharaṁ nitarām avāpa
graiveyakena kim u taṁ tava kaṇṭha-deśaṁ
sampūjayiṣyati punaḥ subhage jano 'yam

Vilāpa-kusumāñjali 33

O beautiful one, when will I be able to worship You with a valuable necklace, which attained all good fortune when it was touched by the arm of Gokulacandra in the festival of the *rāsa* dance?

"O Rādhike! A feast distributing *rasa* is starting in Vṛndāvana. *Rasa* from the heart melts and flows out to be offered to You. Gokulacandra Kṛṣṇa comes and offers You many presentations and pleads that You accept them." But Śrīmatī says, "No! If I take these things, I will be giving Him a chance to come nearby. I will not touch them and I will not let Him near me."

Her *sakhīs* are perplexed, and Kṛṣṇa is very sad, "She won't accept anything from Me?" Lalitā and other *sakhīs* bring Her a flower garland. Rādhārāṇī looks at it and says, "These flowers have no scent or sign of any *sakhī* or *mañjarīs*. They have not picked these flowers or made this garland. This is not from them. It is very harsh, cold, and cruel. I won't touch it. If I touch this, then I will become disturbed. Just the smell already pains Me. Take this garland away from here! Don't bring it near Me. Put it far away on a tree. If the tree becomes happy and honey drops from it, then I will trust it."

But when the *sakhīs* put the garland on a tree, the tree's leaves dry and fall.

"I cannot touch this garland or I will become like that tree," Śrīmatī Rādhārāṇī says.

What is the secret of this garland? This garland had come from the party of Candrāvali. Candrāvali's girlfriends had sent this, hence Rādhārāṇī would not accept it. And when it was placed on the tree favorable to Rādhārāṇī's group, the tree also became disturbed. Therefore Śrīmatī Rādhārāṇī did not touch the garland.

dattaḥ pralamba-ripuṇodbhaṭa-śaṅkhacūḍa-
nāśāt pratoṣi-hṛdayaṁ madhumaṅgalasya
hastena yaḥ sumukhi kaustubha-mitram etaṁ
kiṁ te syamantaka-maṇiṁ taralaṁ kariṣye

Vilāpa-kusumāñjali 34

O beautiful-faced one, when will I make the *syamantaka* jewel, which, after the death of proud Śaṅkhacūḍa was given by Balarāma to cheerful-hearted Madhumaṅgala, who in turn gave it to You, and which since has become the friend of the *kaustubha* jewel, the central jewel in Your necklace?

Once Śaṅkhacūḍa came and attacked the *gopīs*. Kṛṣṇa killed Śaṅkhacūḍa and removed the jewel from his head, giving it to Balarāma, who passed it on to Madhumaṅgala. Madhumaṅgala then gave this to Śrīmatī Rādhārāṇī.

The *sakhīs* pleaded, "Please accept this, then no enemy will be able to look at, touch, or attack You. Kṛṣṇa has sent this jewel to protect You."

"Kṛṣṇa did not send this," Rādhikā replied, "He has come here Himself in the form of this jewel. If I touch this, I will become restless and lose everything. I won't touch it."

Kṛṣṇa, watching from a distance, felt great pain, "Oh! She will not accept anything from Me." He was refused in His attempt for *abhisāra*.

7

The Gold Guard

At the time of chanting, we hold each *tulasī* bead in our *mālā*, like catching the feet of the Vraja-devīs and praying to them as we serve internally. Rādhā-Kṛṣṇa and all the Vraja-devīs are present there while we chant Hare Kṛṣṇa. If we only chant Rādhe Kṛṣṇa, Rādhe means only Śrīmatī Rādhārāṇī, but Hare includes all the *sakhīs* and *mañjarīs*. All the Vraja-devīs are serving Rādhā-Kṛṣṇa in the eternal world. So we pray to them, one by one, as we chant on our *mālā*, "Please give me your tendency to serve, bless me with your moods, and teach me the process by which you serve the Divine Couple. Please guide me and check to see if my actions are wrong or right."

prānta-dvaye parivirājita-guccha-yugma-
vibhrājitena nava-kañcana-ḍorakena
kṣīṇaṁ krudhaty atha kṛśodari ced itīva
badhnāmi bhos tava kadābhibhayena madhyam

Vilāpa-kusumāñjali 35

O slender-waisted one, when, fearing that Your slender waist might break, will I carefully tie it with a new golden belt, splendid with flower-cluster tassels at each end?

Dāsa Gosvāmī says, "You have long hair and Your head is decorated with braids, gold, and jewels. Your body carries a lot of weight, but how can You carry this? O Kiśorī! You have a very thin waist; if this breaks, then what will I do? Therefore I will carefully bind Your waist with a golden belt."

Why does Dāsa Gosvāmī pray to use a gold belt? Gold is beautiful, light and bright, and of a similar color to Rādhārāṇī.

Gold is not selfish; it is like a helpful servant. Gold doesn't leave its post as a servant. If you make a golden ornament, it lasts for a very long time. Even if it breaks, still it can be repaired. Many *sevakas* serve for one or two days, giving cloth, food, water, lodging and so forth, but after a few days they fly off like fireflies. This is not called a *sevaka*. A real *sevaka* is like gold—steady and permanent. A *sevaka* will not be like silver, which may oxidize and lose its potency. Gold doesn't lose its value. Other things may come and mix with gold, but then it can be heated and all other minerals and metals will be burnt out.

kanaka-guṇitam uccair mauktikaṁ mat-karāt te
tila-kusuma-vijetrī nāsikā sā su-vṛttaṁ
madhumathana-mahāli-kṣobhakaṁ hema-gauri
prakaṭatara-maranda-prāyam ādāsyate kim
Vilāpa-kusumāñjali 36

O golden one, when will Your nose, which defeats the sesame flower, receive from my hand a beautiful, golden, honey-pearl that agitates the great bumblebee Kṛṣṇa?

"O Rādhike! Your color is more beautiful and brilliant than molten gold. When a flower blossoms, the bumblebees rush towards it. Your nose is more attractive than a sesame flower. The transcendental bumblebee Kṛṣṇa comes hovering side-to-side, looking for a way to touch Her. To protect You, I will place a nose-ring so Kṛṣṇa cannot come inside. When Kṛṣṇa sees Your nose-ring, He will have a deep desire, 'How can I take the honey from this enchanting flower?' "

aṅgadena tava vāma-doḥ-sthale
svarṇa-gauri nava-ratna-mālikām
paṭṭa-guccha-pariśobhitam imam
ājñayā pariṇayāmi te kadā
Vilāpa-kusumāñjali 37

O golden one, when, by Your order, will I place on Your left arm a silken band, tied with jewels and flowers?

In his perfected body, Dāsa Gosvāmī starts his service from the early morning. Rati Mañjarī combs Rādhārāṇī's hair and decorates it with flowers, jewels, and pearls. She also places a nose ring, bangles, anklebells, anklets, and other ornaments on Śrīmatījī.

karṇayor upari cakra-śalāke
cañcalākṣi nihite mayakā te
kṣobhakaṁ nikhila-gopa-vadhūnāṁ
cakravad bhramayatāṁ mura-śatrum
Vilāpa-kusumāñjali 38

O restless-eyed one, when will I place rings on Your ears that would make Kṛṣṇa, who agitates all the *gopīs*, aimlessly wander in a circle?

Rati Mañjarī then places golden *cakra* wheel-shaped earrings on Rādhārāṇī's ears. Why? These act like Her protectors. If any bad sound comes close, the *cakra* will protect Rādhārāī's ears, telling the sound, "Get out, you are not welcome here. This is not your place."

Kaṁsa once gave training to his soldiers, "When Kṛṣṇa plays the flute, all the cows, calves, *sakhās*, and Vraja-devīs run to Him. This flute has some mystic power. Learn how to play this flute and then we will attract all the Vrajavasīs out of Vraja to Mathurā, and then Kṛṣṇa will be powerless."

Kaṁsa thus opened a flute-training center in Mathurā. When properly trained, Kaṁsa's minions went and played flutes in the forests of Vraja, pretending to be Kṛṣṇa. Hearing this, the cows looked up and thought, "Is Kṛṣṇa calling?" The cows listened intently for a moment. They are very clever. Their ears went to this side and that, drinking the sound of the flute.

But they know the melody of Kṛṣṇa's flute and were not fooled by Kaṁsa's attempted trick. They ignored the flute sound and continued to eat grass without a care. Kaṁsa's minions saw, "Oh, Kṛṣṇa's cows are very clever, they are not listening."

Then they went and played the flute on the bank of the Yamunā, thinking, "The *gopīs* come here to collect water. When they come, we will mesmerize them with our attractive flute playing and will bring them to Mathurā."

But the *gopīs*' ears have these *cakras*, protecting them from antagonistic sounds. Their earrings act like guards, standing at their ears. Therefore the *gopīs* wear Murāri *cakras* in their ears and hair so that only the sound of Kṛṣṇa's flute-call can come in their ears.

Many people send news and many other sounds come, but first-class *sevakas* first check, "Is this good and helpful or not?" as Svarūpa Dāmodara Gosvāmī would first peruse any material for faulty conclusions before he showed it to Mahāprabhu.

kadā te mṛgaśāvākṣi cibuke mṛganābhinā
bindum ullāsayiṣyāmi mukundāmoda-mandire

Vilāpa-kusumāñjali 39

O fawn-eyed one, when will I place a dot of splendid musk on Your chin, the temple of Mukunda's happiness?

Dāsa Gosvāmī prays, "O Rādhike! Your eyes are restless as deer who fear the attack of any dangerous animal or hunter, waiting in a hidden place to shoot. I will decorate Your chin with a spot of musk."

This musk gives power, enthusiasm, and happiness. This spot is dark, like the pupils of Kṛṣṇa's eyes. Seeing this, Kṛṣṇa is overjoyed, "Oh! She has awarded My representative some place on Her face!"

8

A Student of Anurāga

utkhādireṇa nava-candra-virājitena
rāgeṇa te vara-sudhādhara-bimba-yugme
gāṅgeya-gātri mayakā pariraññjite 'smin
daṁśaṁ vidhāsyati haṭhāt kim u kṛṣṇa-kīraḥ
Vilāpa-kusumāñjali 41

O golden-limbed one, when will the Kṛṣṇa-parrot bite the nectarful *bimba* fruits of Your lips, splendid with red *khadira* and camphor, placed by me?

In Vraja-maṇḍala there are many parrots that sport many beautiful shades of green and blue, and their beaks are red, yellow, or brown. Their necks have an enchanting reddish ring, looking like they are wearing a necklace. With their restless eyes, the parrots are always searching, "Where are the ripe fruits?" They seek the biggest and sweetest fruits hidden among the clusters of leaves. They fly very quickly, bite the fruit, drink its juice, and come back. They do not eat the whole fruit, only a small part, and they never touch a fruit that has already been tasted. In Vraja-maṇḍala there is one parrot in particular that is famous, but He does not fly. If anyone invites Him, remembers Him or calls out to Him, He first considers, "Is this sweet for Me or not?" At that time, there is one guardian without whose order He will not touch or look at a fruit. Is He hungry or thirsty? No! He is never hungry or thirsty, He already has everything.

Gaṅgā-devī's body is Her water. She is pure and clear. When the sun rises in the early morning, the sunshine turns the water crimson. At this time, the fish in the water become bewildered and think that juicy fruits have appeared in the water, seeing the reddish light sparkling in the river. Then the fish drink so much water, thinking it is very sweet. Why? Because of its color. In the evening, when the sun sets, this color is also there.

If anyone's heart is colored with *anurāga*, he will appear to be lit up by the crimson tinge of the sunrise. Then he will be attractive to all living beings. If anyone thinks of Kṛṣṇa, brings Kṛṣṇa in his heart, and plays with Him there, Kṛṣṇa knows this person is ready for Him to come and taste his love, like a fruit ripe with *anurāga*.

Young unripe fruit are green in color. When the sun gives heat, they grow and become big and ripe. They turn crimson and a wonderful fragrance comes from them. The sun is like a parent who helps the fruits grow, and when they are mature, he calls the parrot to come and meet with them, giving an indication, "This fruit is now ripe, go and taste it."

The Vraja-devīs' hearts are pure, like the glistening water of Gaṅgā-devī lit crimson by the sun. They have millions of good qualities. Those who bathe in the waters of Gaṅgā-devī are purified and refreshed. But the limbs of the Vraja-devīs are millions of times purer than even Gaṅgā-devī.

Kṛṣṇa Śuka always moves about in search of nectar. When He sees that the Vraja-devīs' lips and cheeks have a crimson hue, His target is apparent. They are in fresh youth, and a wonderful aroma exuding from their bodies attracts the parrot Kṛṣṇa, who appears to fly there. He kisses them and then runs off.

Kṛṣṇa Śuka wanders throughout Vraja-maṇḍala, examining everyone. If anyone likes Him, He will go to that person. He will go to those who carry Him in their heart. He checks, "Have they really offered themselves to Me or not?" If they have completely offered themselves to Him, He then goes and kisses them, making them even sweeter, just like when a parrot increases the sweetness of a fruit by biting it with its beak.

yat-prānta-deśa-lava-leśa-vighūrṇitena
baddhaḥ kṣaṇād bhavati kṛṣṇa-karīndra uccaiḥ
tat-khañjarīta-jayi-netra-yugaṁ kadāyaṁ
sampūjayiṣyati janas tava kajjalena

Vilāpa-kusumāñjali 42

When will this person worship with black *kājala* Your two eyes, which defeat the *khañjana* birds, and which, with the slightest movement from their corners, in a moment tightly bind the regal elephant Kṛṣṇa?

The eyes of Śrīmatī Rādhāränī and the Vraja-devīs are long and tinged crimson. They are afflicted by restlessness. Wishing to cool Śrīmatī Rādhārānī's eyes, Dāsa Gosvāmī says, "I will decorate Your eyes with *kājala*." Why? Her eyes are always searching for Kṛṣṇa. If this black ointment is there, then She will feel pacified and think that Kṛṣṇa is close to Her eyes.

Kṛṣṇa is like an elephant. An elephant has a large body but small eyes. Kṛṣṇa's vision is one-pointed. He does not see other's faults. He only looks for love. "Who loves Me?" He says to Himself, as He searches for a sign. He looks for those who wear a dark sari or who put *kājala* on their eyes, indicating, "I am inviting You. Come stay in My eyes." Receiving a sign like this, Kṛṣṇa Śuka will come to meet such a person. He will not go without some invitation.

Dāsa Gosvāmi says, "Knowing that Kṛṣṇa will not come without a sign, I will arrange everything. I will lovingly anoint Your eyes with *kājala*, as a signal for Kṛṣṇa. Kṛṣṇa will then understand that we are welcoming Him."

yasyāṅka-rañjita-śiras tava-māna-bhaṅge
goṣṭhendra-sūnur adhikaṁ suṣamam upaiti
lakṣā-rasaḥ sa ca kadā padayor adhas te
nyasto mayāpy atitarāṁ chavim āpsyatīha
Vilāpa-kusumāñjali 43

When will Your lotus feet shine with splendor as Kṛṣṇa is beautified by anointing His head with the reddish mark from Your feet which I decorated with lac, in His efforts to soothe Your jealous anger?

Sometimes Śrīmatī feels *māna* when She sees that Kṛṣṇa is joking and talking with other *sakhīs* and teaching them how to serve Her. Although He means well, He has come and taught them without Her permission. The *sakhīs* and *mañjarīs* come to Rādhārānī with the knowledge they have received from Kṛṣṇa. When a *sakhī* comes and tries to decorate Rādhārānī with the process Kṛṣṇa taught, Śrīmatī Rādhārānī asks, "How did you learn to do this kind of decoration? Who is your teacher?"

"Oh, I learnt this at Sakhī Giri," the *sakhī* says, "one teacher came there and taught me how to make these kinds of designs on the hands. The stones there are quite amazing. We practiced on the stones, and then the marks would not wash off."

"Oh, show me this at Sakhī Giri," Rādhārānī says. They go there and see many designs imprinted on the stones. Rādhārānī understands who made these designs and says, "You have learned from a bogus teacher. I will not take any of your *sevā*. Learn from Me. I will teach you." Then She begins instructing them.

They go to another stone at Sakhī Giri. With color on Her hand, Śrīmātījī touches the stone. The stone becomes very soft at Her touch. It brings the print of Her hand in its heart and keeps it there as its treasure.

The *sakhīs* and *mañjarīs* then decorate Śrīmātī's feet with *alta* and *kuṁkum*. They notice that whenever Her feet touch a stone, the designs on Her feet stay there on its surface. Even after washing it, the stone does not give up the sign. How is this stone so soft and sweet? This hill, called Sakhī Giri, carries signs from the Vraja-devīs' and Kṛṣṇa's feet. Śrīmatī personally teaches the *sakhīs* not only the art of decorating feet and hands, but also how to play musical instruments. There are many stones there that make musical notes when tapped in different ways. Rādhārāṇī plays music on these specially empowered stones.

But first She had *māna*, "Who is this so-called *guru* in Vraja? I will not accept anything from one who takes training from Him." From that day there was only one *guru* among the *gopīs*. Who? Viśākhā-devī was instructed by Rādhārāṇī to teach the Vraja-devīs.

Nanda-nandana Kṛṣṇa Himself then applied to study at Sakhī Giri under the tutorship of Viśākhā-devī. At His request for enrollment, the *sakhīs* said to Him, "We will admit You on one condition. You must wear a *sari*. We will comb and decorate Your hair with flowers and place bangles and ornaments on Your body, only then can You become our student."

Kṛṣṇa agreed and the Vraja-devīs dressed and decorated Him, and then drew designs on His hands. When they were done, He said, "I must now take My examination. I will touch one of these stones. If it accepts My handprint, I will understand that I have been trained well."

Kṛṣṇa went and placed His hand on a stone, but it did not accept His touch. "This is not good," He said, "you aren't qualified teachers. I need a qualified tutor." Dāsa Gosvāmī says, "I will bring Kṛṣṇa to Śrīmatī Rādhārāṇī." She will tell Him, 'First bathe in Dehī-kuṇḍa and then come back." Kṛṣṇa went and bathed there, becoming completely clean.

When He returned, He prostrated Himself before Rādhārāṇī and begged for Her mercy, saying:

smara-garala-khaṇḍanaṁ mama śirasi maṇḍanaṁ
dehi pada-pallavam-udāraṁ

Śrī Gīta-govinda 10.8

O My beloved, Cupid's powerful poison is devastating Me. Please be merciful and place upon My head the cooling, tender petals of Your lotus feet.

Śrīmatī Rādhārāṇī placed Her feet on Kṛṣṇa's head, blessing His head with the reddish marks on Her lotus feet. She then accepted Him as a student of *anurāga*.

A pupil that is not surrendered to his teacher cannot learn anything. Disciples come to Gurudeva, but he can only teach them if they actually desire to learn. If a so-called student has no relation, connection, or affection for his *guru* and no desire to accept what his *guru* is offering, then receiving knowledge is impossible. Although it seems he may be studying and learning, nothing will stay with him. If there is a good relationship between *guru* and disciple, tutor and student, then all the master's teachings can come within the heart of the pupil and remain there forever.

If you are a so-called disciple who comes and sits in class, while having no relation with the Ācārya, and no desire to learn, then the teaching will go to you, bounce off, and then go to another.

Viśākhā and Lalitā administer one last examination. They tell Kṛṣṇa to walk on the stones, and as He does so, the stones manifest His imprint on their smooth surfaces. The stones confirm that Kṛṣṇa is now surrendered.

Today, Śrīmatī Rādhārāṇī's *māna* was pacified when She saw that Kṛṣṇa was completely surrendered to Her.

Kṛṣṇa then decorated Rādhārāṇī's feet with *alta* and *kuṁkum*. Sakhī Giri gives this evidence. This Sakhī Giri hill is therefore very special and helpful.

kalāvati natāṁsayoḥ pracura-kāma-puñjojjvalat-
kalānidhi-muradviṣaḥ prakaṭa-rāsa-sambhāvayoḥ
bhrama-bhramara-jhaṅkṛtair madhura-malli-mālāṁ
mudā kadā tava tayoḥ samarpayati devi dāsī-janaḥ
Vilāpa-kusumāñjali 44

O graceful artist, O Devī, when will this maidservant happily place a sweet jasmine garland, filled with the humming of bees, on Your gracefully sloping shoulders, touched in the *rāsa* dance by Muradviṣa, who has become a moon shining with amorous passion?

Dāsa Gosvāmī prays, "O Devī, You are expert in the sixty-four arts. Kṛṣṇa also knows all arts. Therefore, at the time of *rāsa-līlā*, He sings, dances, and moves to each *gopī*, attracting and meeting with each of them. With sixty-four qualities I will make a garland, and will offer this to You. You can then offer it to Kṛṣṇa at the time of the *rāsa-līlā*. When this garland touches Kṛṣṇa, He will think, 'This garland is so sweet, made with the choicest flowers, and full of all good qualities.' "

At the time of making the flower garland, a bumblebee came and sang, "This garland is bright, light, and attractive. If you offer this to Kṛṣṇa, He will be very pleased."

A strong flow of water comes down from the source of any great river. When a strong flow of air meets with the water's flow, their meeting causes whirlpools to spin about in the river. These whirlpools send up a fine mist that hangs suspended on both sides of the river and cools all residents nearby, making them feel refreshed and joyful.

Dāsa Gosvāmī says, "I am a very small servant, but I will collect the mercy and qualities of the *sakhīs* and *mañjarīs*, and will place them inside the garland I offer to You. On each flower I will write the holy names of the *sakhīs* and *mañjarīs* with sandal paste, *aguru*, and *kastūrī*. You can give this garland to Kṛṣṇa."

The *mañjarīs* do not make dry and plain garlands. A garland is not made of paper or artificial flowers. The *gopīs* do everything with the greatest care and love.

sūryāya sūryamaṇi-nirmita-vedi-madhye
mugdhāṅgi bhāvata ihāli-kulair vṛtāyāḥ
arghaṁ samarpayitum utka-dhiyas tavārāt
sajjāni kiṁ sumukhi dāsyati dāsikeyam

Vilāpa-kusumāñjali 45

O charming-limbed one, O lovely faced beauty, when will this maidservant hand You the articles of worship when, surrounded by Your friends, You are eager at heart to devotedly offer *argha* to the Sun-god, on an altar of *sūryamaṇi* jewels?

Dāsa Gosvāmī now says, "Jewels like the *sūryamaṇi* give off light and are powerful, but have no sweet scent. The *kaustubha maṇi* meets with Kṛṣṇa and is His dear friend, but this garland I make is endowed with the specialties of the sixty-four arts. It is infused with the qualities, fragrance, and heartfelt love of all the *sakhīs*. I will arrange that garland and give it to You. Then at the time of *rāsa-līlā*, You will give this to Kṛṣṇa. By this, both of You will transfer Your heartfelt love."

Here, *sumukhi* means *sevonmukhi*. A person's face is sweet if he is always inclined to serve. If someone has no service tendency, if his heart is dry, then anywhere he goes, he will only suffer. Why? You have no desire to accept anything. When will desire for service come? If we have a desire to serve and accept something, then the residents of Vraja will give a spark of their service tendency, desire, and mood.

Now we don't pray for anything. We say, "*Manasī-sevā* is speculation; this is all bogus." We have no hope. If we are not greedy for pure love, and have no hope, then how can that pure love come and bless us? Nothing will come!

Dāsa Gosvāmī says, "O Rādhe, You are *sumukhi*, Your face is so attractive. You are the embodiment of all love and service tendency. I am Your small maidservant, but my desires are very big. I am Your *sevonmukhi-dasī*."

Young people dream of what they will be when they grow up. They have high expectations, and think, "I will be a big barrister," or "I will be a famous architect," or "I will be a lawyer practicing in the Supreme Court." They have big hopes from their childhood. As ordinary people have greed for ordinary achievements, we must develop spiritual greed for extraordinary, spiritual achievements. If we have no spiritual greed or desire, nor any hope to achieve any aspiration, our life is only like an empty shell. We are not really human; we are impotent and like a stone or inert object.

People cheat others, saying, "*Mānasī-sevā* is speculation." When a baby is born, after some time it becomes natural for the baby to ask questions. They soak up information. Even before a baby goes to school, he starts inquiring from his parents about all kinds of things, saying, "Mama, what is this? Papa, what is that?"

If we don't go and pray to the Guru-varga for spiritual instruction, if we have no scent of greed, how can we be called students of the spiritual science? Are we humans? Are we trunks of wood or chunks of stone? Who are we? The soul is the part and parcel of the Supreme Soul. It has consciousness, but in its perverted state, this consciousness is now absorbed in dull matter. When a ray of divine mercy touches the soul by earnest prayer, then greed arises for attaining the pure state of consciousness in love with the Supreme.

Dāsa Gosvāmī is Rati Mañjarī in the spiritual world. She is *sevonmukhi*, always eager to serve the Divine Couple. This tendency is born naturally out of her love. She prays, "O Śrīmatī Rādhike, I am Your small maidservant. I will make a flower seat for You in the forest of Vṛndāvana. You will sit there happily and worship the sun. You will offer *argha* and other paraphernalia to the sun. You are *sumukhi-sevonmukhi*, always serving and teaching others how to serve.

"I will make a jeweled seat for You. And from there, You can serve Mitradeva with the *sakhīs*. The sun is coming! He rises early. But He will take some time to reach here, therefore we must prepare for His arrival. O *sumukhi, sevonmukhi*! Be pleased with this *dāsī* and give her inspiration and instructions for service. This *dāsī* of Yours will arrange everything for the service of the Sun-god. When the sun-like Kṛṣṇa arises and comes here and accepts Your presentations, then the arrangement made by Your *sakhīs* will be successful. I will prepare all things for that worship. I have no good intelligence; I don't know what is needed to perfect this worship. With Your inspiration, I will go to the *sakhīs* and *mañjarīs* and they will guide me in this service."

vraja-pura-pati-rājñyā ājñayā miṣṭam annaṁ
bahu-vidham ati-yatnāt svena pakvaṁ varoru
sapadi nija-sakhīnāṁ mad-vidhānāṁ ca hastair
madhumathana-nimittaṁ kiṁ tvayā sannidhāpyam

Vilāpa-kusumāñjali 46

O lovely-thighed one, when, employing the hands of Your friends such as myself, will You place before the killer of the Madhu demon the many delicious foods You very carefully cooked by the order of the queen of Vraja?

"O Rādhike! On the request of Yaśodā Mātā, You arrange and cook many sweets, such as *halavā, laḍḍu, kṣīra-sāgara,* and *kṣīri.* I am Your Rati Mañjarī. I will take something for Kṛṣṇa and give it to Yaśodā Mātā, saying, 'O Yaśodā Mātā, please give this to Kṛṣṇa. Śrīmatījī has made this with Her own hands. It is very tasty, sweet, and helpful for Kṛṣṇa.' "

Yaśodā Mātā gives the *gopīs* the chance to serve Kṛṣṇa. Rādhārānī cooks with Lalitā and all the *sakhīs* and *mañjarīs* in the kitchen of Nandagrāma. And She gives what She cooks to Rati Mañjarī, saying, "Go give this to Yaśodā Mātā."

Why does Śrīmatī Rādhārānī entrust this offering to Rati Mañjarī? Because anything Rati Mañjarī gives is completely filled with love. She is none other than the personified form of Śrīmatī Rādhārānī's affection for Kṛṣṇa. Rati Mañjarī knows the process of offering the preparations.

9

Merciful Remnants

nītānna-mad-vidha-lalāṭa-taṭe lalāṭaṁ
prītyā pradāya muditā vraja-rāja-rājñī
premṇā prasūr iva bhavat-kuśalasya pṛcchāṁ
bhāvye vidhāsyati kadā mayi tāvakatvāt

Vilāpa-kusumāñjali 47

O beautiful one, when, lovingly touching her forehead to mine, will the jubilant queen of Vraja, Yaśodā Mātā, like a loving mother ask me about Your welfare, because I am Your maidservant?

Dāsa Gosvāmī prays, "O Rādhe, You are the source and original form of all auspiciousness. I long for the day when the queen of Vraja, Yaśodā, receives the preparations I carry to her. Becoming pleased with me, she will catch my hand and say, "Oh, you are Rādhārānī's dearest *mañjarī*!" With the love of a mother for her own daughter, she will kiss my forehead and stroke her hands through my hair. "You are very dear to Rādhārānī," she will say. "Your love is very sweet. Kṛṣṇa is so pleased with anything you bring from Her and He eats it with great relish."

Śrīmatī Rādhārānī's cooking is *maṅgala-svarūpa*, the abode of all auspiciousness. It is unfathomably tasteful and famous throughout the three worlds.

Yaśodā Mātā is so pleased with Śrīmatī Rādhārānī's *sakhīs* and *mañjarīs*, but she has special affection for Rati Mañjarī. Rati Mañjarī knows how to keep Śrīmatī Rādhārānī's cooking fresh, hot, and unseen by others before it reaches mother Yaśodā and Kṛṣṇa. Her desire is pure and selfless. Yaśodā Mātā sees this love.

kṛṣṇa-vaktrāmbujocchiṣṭaṁ
prasādaṁ param ādarāt
dattaṁ dhaniṣṭhayā devi
kim āneṣyāmi te 'grataḥ

Vilāpa-kusumāñjali 48

O Devī, when will I place before You Kṛṣṇa's remnants which are respectfully brought by Dhaniṣṭhā-gopī?

When Kṛṣṇa eats, He leaves some remnants. Yaśodā Mātā tells Dhaniṣṭhā, "Kṛṣṇa's plate has some leftover pieces of sweets and other foodstuffs. Go collect His remnants." Dhanisṭhā, who is expert in all kinds of tricky maneuvers, somehow slips Kṛṣṇa's remnants to Rati Mañjarī. Rati Mañjarī then gives it to Rūpa Mañjarī, who gives it to Lalitā-devī, who gives it to Śrīmatī Rādhārānī. After Rādhārānī has tasted Kṛṣṇa's remnants, all the *sakhīs* and *mañjarīs* take some of this *prasāda*. Only they can understand how sweet that *mahā-prasāda* is.

nānā-vidhair amṛta-sāra-rasāyanais
taiḥ kṛṣṇa-prasāda-militair iha bhojya-peyaiḥ
hā kuṅkumāṅgi lalitādi-sakhī-vṛtā tvaṁ
yatnān mayā kim u tarām upabhojanīyā

Vilāpa-kusumāñjali 49

O You whose limbs are anointed with *kuṁkum*, when will I carefully feed You, Lalitā and Your other friends many kinds of food and nectar drinks, mixed with the remnants of what was directly tasted by Lord Kṛṣṇa?

Once, during Raghunātha Dāsa Gosvāmī's meditation, he cooked sweet rice with almonds, ghee, honey, and saffron. In his eternal form as Rati Mañjarī, he offered this sweet rice to Rūpa Mañjarī, who gave it to Śrīmatī Rādhārānī, who gave it to Kṛṣṇa.

After Rādhā-Kṛṣṇa tasted the *ksīra*, They asked Lalita-devī who had cooked it, and hearing it was Rati Mañjarī, They told her to take some to Rati so that she could taste how wonderful the *ksīra* was. The *mañjarīs* happily fed Rati Mañjarī the remnants of the *ksīra* she had cooked. In the evening, Raghunātha dāsa Gosvāmī suffered from wind in his bowels because he was not used to eating almond *ksīra*. The question comes: After taking *kṛṣṇa-prasāda*, how can anyone suffer any disturbance?

The *Bhagavad-gītā* (2.65) states:

prasāde sarva-duḥkhānāṁ hānir asyopajāyate
prasanna-cetaso hy āśu buddhiḥ paryavatiṣṭhate

When one receives *prasāda*, all his miseries are dispelled. His intelligence becomes content and he feels full of bliss.

Prasāda destroys all suffering and causes its receiver to feel great joy. Then why did Dāsa Gosvāmī's stomach become full of gas by taking this *ksīra mahā-prasāda*? It was cooked with milk, almonds, pure ghee, and honey, and was tasted by Kṛṣṇa, Śrīmatī Rādhārānī, and the *sakhīs* and *mañjarīs*. To teach that *mānasī-sevā* is not mere speculation, Kṛṣṇa arranged this pastime to happen.

A doctor was called and checked Dāsa Gosvāmī's condition. "The Bābā has eaten almond *ksīra*," he concluded.

The local people did not believe him. "What are you saying? He only takes one cup of buttermilk a day," they said.

Rādhārānī has very deep love for Rati Mañjarī. She offers Her love, or *rati*, to Kṛṣṇa. Whenever Kṛṣṇa takes *prasādam*, He leaves something for Rādhārānī.

After Caitanya Mahāprabhu accepted Raghunātha dāsa Gosvāmī in Jagannātha Purī and offered him to Svarūpa Dāmodara, Dāsa Gosvāmī would regularly invite Mahāprabhu and all the devotees to come for a feast. Mahāprabhu and His associates would come and take *praśāda* on Dāsa Gosvāmī's request. This went on for two or three years, and then suddenly Raghunātha dāsa Gosvāmī stopped sending invitations.

Mahāprabhu inquired, "Why has Raghunātha stopped the feasts?"

"Raghunātha says that You go there and take *praśādam* on his request," Svarūpa Dāmodara said, "but internally You are not pleased. He does everything for Your pleasure. Knowing You were not happy within, he has stopped this program."

"Yes," Mahāprabhu said, "Raghunātha has understood My heart and mind.

> *viṣayīra anna khāile malina haya mana*
> *malina mana haile, nahe kṛṣṇera smaraṇa*
> *Caitanya-caritāmṛta, Antya-līlā* 6.278

> When one eats food offered by sensuous or worldly people the mind becomes contaminated, and in that state one cannot remember Kṛṣṇa.

Why was Mahāprabhu disturbed? These feasts were arranged with the money from Govardhana Majūmadāra, the wealthy father of Raghunātha dāsa Gosvāmī, and therefore fell under the category of eatables mentioned in the above verse.

Some days later, Mahāprabhu asked Svarūpa Dāmodara, "How does Raghunātha maintain his life?"

Svarūpa Dāmodara said, "He waits outside the gate of Jagannātha's temple to be given some alms. Some people give him some food and he maintains his life by taking that."

Some time later, Mahāprabhu said, "I have not seen Raghunātha by the gate of the temple for many days. Now how does he sustain his life?"

"Raghunātha says that the kind of begging that he was doing was pertaining to the nature of a prostitute. In this position, one waits and looks expectantly, hoping that a person will give something. As the people pass by one after the other, one wonders, 'Will he give? Will he give?' He says he will no longer do this. Now he simply goes to a charity center and accepts just enough to maintain his life."

After some more days, Mahāprabhu asked Svarūpa Dāmodara, "What is Raghunātha doing now to sustain his life?"

"He is no longer going to the charity center, declaring that the food there is provided by enjoyers; that it has been bought and distributed by worldly people. Now he eats the leftover *mahā-praśāda* from the drain area of the Jagannātha Temple. Raghunātha collects leftover *mahā-prasāda* that has been rejected by the cows and other animals. He washes it and eats a small amount to maintain his life."

Outside the Jagannātha temple, there are large areas where leftover *mahā-prasāda* is placed and is eaten by cows, dogs, and pigs.

One day, Caitanya Mahāprabhu went to see the exalted faith of Raghunātha in *mahā-prasāda*. The Lord watched from a hidden place as Raghunātha washed the *mahā-prasāda* and prepared to take some.

Suddenly, Mahāprabhu ran forward and caught his hand, saying, "You are very selfish. You are taking this supremely tasteful *mahā-prasāda* without giving Me any!"

Mahāprabhu then took a handful and ate it. When He went to take a second handful, Svarūpa Dāmodara caught His hand and stopped Him.

"Raghunātha's renunciation is like lines etched on a stone," Mahāprabhu said. "It is breaking My heart. I cannot tolerate this."

Mahāprabhu later told Govinda Prabhu, "From now on, after I take *prasāda*, divide the remaining amount into three parts, one for you, one for Haridāsa, and one for Raghunātha."

How much love Mahāprabhu has for Raghunātha dāsa

Gosvāmī! Later, Mahāprabhu gave Raghunātha dāsa Gosvāmī a Govardhana-*śilā* and a *guñjā-mālā* to worship. Mahāprabhu also gave him a special instruction:

grāmya-kathā nā śunibe, grāmya-vārtā nā kahibe
bhāla nā khāibe āra bhāla nā paribe
amānī mānada hañā kṛṣṇa-nāma sadā la'be
vraje rādhā-kṛṣṇa-sevā mānase karibe
Caitanya-caritāmṛta, Antya-līlā 6.236–237

Do not talk like people in general or hear what they say. Do not eat very palatable food, nor dress very nicely. Do not expect honor, but offer all respect to others. Always chant the holy name of Kṛṣṇa, and within your mind render service to Rādhā and Kṛṣṇa in Vṛndāvana.

Mahāprabhu instructed Dāsa Gosvāmī to begin *mānasī-sevā* and he followed this very diligently.

pānāya vari madhuraṁ nava-pātalādi-
karpūra-vāsitataraṁ taralākṣi dattvā
kāle kadā tava mayācamanīya-danta-
kaṣṭādikaṁ praṇayataḥ param arpaṇīyam
Vilāpa-kusumāñjali 50

O restless-eyed one, when will I lovingly give You sweet drinking water, scented with fresh *pātala* flowers and camphor, to rinse Your mouth, along with a toothbrush-twig, and other articles?

Dāsa Gosvāmī prays to offer a fragrant mouthwash for Śrīmatī Rādhārānī, along with other paraphernalia for Her service, like a twig for brushing Her teeth. The *sakhīs* and *mañjarīs* also prepare this for Kṛṣṇa under the guidance of Śrīmatījī. They put water in a clay pot and it becomes cooled. On top of the pot they place a cloth, and put roses or jasmine and other flowers on that cloth, and then bind another cloth on top. The next morning, that water will have a wonderful smell, and will be pure and fresh. Then they give that water to clean Kṛṣṇa's teeth and to use for *ācamana*. They also give a soft cotton cloth to dry His hands and mouth.

bhojanasya samaye tava yatnād
devi dhūpa-nivahān vara-gandhān
vījanādyam api tat-kṣaṇa-yogyaṁ
hā kadā praṇayataḥ praṇayāmi
Vilāpa-kusumāñjali 51

O Devī, when, with great love, will I carefully light an abundance of incense, fan You, and perform other suitable services as You take Your meal?"

Dāsa Gosvāmī prays, "While You take *prasāda*, I will arrange incense and perfume to make the area aromatic. I will decorate the area with flowers and will fan You as You eat."

Dāsa Gosvāmī also prays to be able to fan Kṛṣṇa as He eats, saying, "You gave me instruction for this service and You directly taught me how to fan Kṛṣṇa." Then, due to the fragrance and flowing air, Kṛṣṇa will peacefully take *prasāda*.

10

Adharāmṛta

karpūra-pūra-paripūrita-nāga-valli-
parṇādi-pūga-parikalpita-vīṭikaṁ te
vaktrāmbuje madhura-gātri mudā kadāhaṁ
protphulla-roma-nikaraiḥ param arpayāmi

Vilāpa-kusumāñjali 52

O sweet-limbed one, when, the hairs of my body standing upright in ecstasy, will I place a betel-leaf, filled with betel nuts and camphor, into Your mouth?

Dāsa Gosvāmī prays to offer *tāmbūla* with betel nuts, clove, camphor, and spices to Śrīmatī Rādhārāṇī. Vṛndā-Devī's garden has many creepers and plants. All different kinds of spices grow in Vṛndāvana. The *tāmbūla* in Vṛndāvana-dhāma is of a special nature. It grows in shady places, and doesn't like to meet with the sun. The *tāmbūla* creepers are very shy. They are only born for the service of Rādhā-Kṛṣṇa. They don't like to remain exposed thinking that people will see and pick them. If anything comes and meets with these creepers, it is as if the creepers wilt and die. In its favorable environment, the *tāmbūla* grows large, thick leaves, which are very tasty. They are not too sweet, bitter, or hot. These leaves are reserved by the Vraja-devīs for Kṛṣṇa and Śrīmatī Rādhārāṇī. They wrap betel nuts, cloves, saffron, and other spices in these leaves. Rati Mañjarī gives these to Śrīmatī Rādhārāṇī, and She offers them to Kṛṣṇa. Because Rati Mañjarī has boundless love for Rādhā-Kṛṣṇa, the *sakhīs* have deep affection for her and give her many opportunities to serve.

Tāmbūla aids digestion, and colors Kṛṣṇa's lips and tongue reddish. By chewing *tāmbūla*, the voice becomes very sweet. It makes Kṛṣṇa's tone and melody sweet, so that He can play the flute and sing even more beautifully.

ārātrikeṇa bhavatīṁ kim u devi devīṁ
nirmañchayiṣyatitarāṁ lalitā pramodāt
anyālayaś ca nava-maṅgala-gāna-puṣpaiḥ
prāṇārbudair api kacair api dāsikeyam
Vilāpa-kusumāñjali 53

O Devī, O beloved of Kṛṣṇa, at the time when Lalitā worships You with an *ārati* lamp, as Your other friends worship You with auspicious new songs and flowers, will this maidservant, thinking You millions of times more dear than her own life's breath, worship You with her hair?

Lalitā-devī arranges Rādhā-Kṛṣṇa's *ārati*. The main *āratis* occur three times a day—in the morning, afternoon, and evening. There are an additional two *āratis*: *śṛṅgāra-ārati* and *śayana-āratī*. At the time of *ārati* the *gopīs* sing of Rādhā-Kṛṣṇa's qualities and offer Them flowers. These flowers are all conscious souls eager to be engaged in the service of the Divine Couple. Lalitā-devī offers incense, a lamp, water, and flowers. *Śṛṅgāra-rasa*, or *madhura-rasa*, has five kinds of relations—*sakhī, nitya-sakhī, prāṇa-sakhī, priya-sakhī*, and *priya-narma-sakhī*. The five groups of *sakhīs* offer their loving moods in the form of different articles such as incense, ghee lamp, water, flowers, *tulasī, candana*, and a fan. The *sakhīs* and *mañjarīs* offer their love in the form of *ārati*. Kṛṣṇa accepts their love and returns it.

The *sakhīs* sing *maṅgala-gāṇa*. While performing this auspicious singing they offer each article. This is more pleasing than any ornament that can be offered. Kṛṣṇa drinks the nectar of their singing with His ears and keeps it in His heart. He is very greedy to hear the *gopīs*' singing and will not get up until *maṅgala-āratī* is arranged. He waits to hear this singing and, receiving this nectar, He feels energized and is overjoyed.

The *gopīs*' hair is very sweet and lovely. There is a special beauty in their hair. Dāsa Gosvāmī says that he will offer *ārati* with his hair.

ālī-kulena lalitā-pramukhena sārdham
ātanvatī tvaṁ iha nirbhara-narma-goṣṭhīm
mat-pāṇi-kalpita-manohara-keli-talpam
ābhūṣayiṣyasi kadā svapanena devi
Vilāpa-kusumāñjali 54

O Devī, under the guidance of Your *sakhīs*, headed by Lalitā, I will make a beautiful playbed for You with my own hands. When will You adorn that bed by dreaming on it?

Dāsa Gosvāmī prays, "O Devī, when will I arrange for Your *vilāsa* with Your beloved in the pleasure groves of Vraja? I will make a bed out of flower petals in Vilāsa-kuñja for You to rest on."

The *sakhīs* and *mañjarīs* arrange the Divine Couple's bed out of flower petals. The *gopīs* place freshly blossomed flower petals, which are soft and fragrant like their hearts, on the bed. This increases Kṛṣṇa's greed to rest there with Śrīmatījī.

Lalitā and the other *sakhīs* make an intricate flower decoration above this enchanting bed.

Kṛṣṇa thinks, "I will go and rest there," but He can't find the right pathway. "How can I sit or lay there?" On top there is a cover made of a thin layer of flowers. But beneath the cover, one or two feet down, there is a *kuñja-kuṭīra* hidden below. On four sides the *gopīs* make flower decorations, and in the middle there is a covering of flowers.

"How to go inside? Is there a door? Where is it?" Kṛṣṇa becomes perplexed. The *sakhīs* and *mañjarīs* make newer and newer kinds of *kuñja-kuṭīras* every day.

Kṛṣṇa is surprised, "How do they arrange this? Who gave them such intelligence?"

Sometimes they design the *kuñja-kuṭīra* with a hidden room on top, in which they arrange the bed. Sometimes the sitting places are in the middle or hidden on the side. Kṛṣṇa can't understand what to do. He goes inside the *kuñja*, but can't find where to go. Śrīmatī Rādhārānī is hiding there, waiting to see how clever Kṛṣṇa is.

The *sakhīs* and *mañjarīs* do not disclose the secrets of their design and other services. No one knows how to serve like this. They keep everything secret and hidden; hence they are called *gopīs*. Their hearts are deep and full of love, and their intelligence is also immense.

samvāhayiṣyati padau tava kiṅkarīyaṁ
hā rūpa-mañjarir asau ca karāmbuje dve
yasmin manojña-hṛdaye sadaye 'nayoḥ kiṁ
śrīmān bhaviṣyatitarāṁ śubha-vāsaraḥ saḥ

Vilāpa-kusumāñjali 55

O merciful one, O beautiful-hearted one, when will the auspicious time come that this maidservant massages Your feet and Rūpa Mañjarī massages Your lotus hands?

Rūpa Mañjarī is expert in massaging and is famous for this throughout Vraja-maṇḍala. Many *dāsīs* and *mañjarīs* are all present, but who will get the chance to directly serve Rādhā and Kṛṣṇa?

Dāsa Gosvāmī prays, "I will petition Rūpa Mañjarī to bestow this service upon me. May she accept me and say, 'O *kiṅkarī*, come with me. I will now give you a chance to serve Rādhārāṇī.'

If we don't learn how to serve in *anugatya* then everything we do will be incorrect. Our every action must be performed under guidance for it to be proper.

tavodgīrṇaṁ bhojyaṁ sumukhi kila kallola-salilaṁ
tathā pādāmbhojāmṛtam iha mayā bhakti-latayā

ayi premṇā sārdhaṁ praṇayi-jana-vargair bahu-vidhai
raho labdhavyaṁ kiṁ pracuratara-bhāgyodaya-balaiḥ
Vilāpa-kusumāñjali 56

O lovely-faced one, when will I, on the strength of some great fortune, in a secret place with Your affectionate friends, attain the remnants You had spit out and the waves of nectarful water that washed Your lotus feet and which nourish the *bhakti* creeper?

Dāsa Gosvāmī prays, "When will my good fortune arise and I will taste the remnants Kṛṣṇa has first chewed and then given to Rādhārāṇī? After Rādhārāṇī's *abhiṣeka*, I will collect Her *caraṇāmṛta* and honor it."

This is the most potent nectar for the *bhakti-latā*, the creeper of devotion. Rūpa Mañjarī is always helpful and shares the nectar she collects with all the other *mañjarīs*. This is the nature of friendship among devotees. They always share in Kṛṣṇa's service.

When taking the sweet smelling *tāmbūla* remnants from Śrīmatī Rādhārāṇī and honoring Her footbath water, the *mañjarīs* become completely infused with *anurāga* and their bodies assume a reddish glow.

bhojanāvasare devi snehena sva-mukhāmbujā
mahyaṁ tvad-gata-cittāyai iṁ sudhās tvaṁ pradāsyasi
Vilāpa-kusumāñjali 57

O Devī, during Your meal, will You take some nectar from Your own lotus mouth and lovingly give it me, whose heart has been offered to You?

Dāsa Gosvāmī says, "O Devī Rādhike, at the time of eating, when will You, with great affection, give Your nectarful remnants to this maidservant?"

11

Culinary Perfection

In the fifty-eighth verse of *Vilāpa-kusumāñjali*, Dāsa Gosvāmī prays:

api bata rasavatyāḥ siddhaye mādhavasya
vraja-pati-puram udyad-roma-romā vrajantī
skhalita-gatir udañcat-svānta-saukhyena kiṁ me
kvacid api nayanābhyāṁ lāpsyase svāmini tvam

Vilāpa-kusumāñjali 58

O Devī, while You are on Your way to the home of the king of Vraja, to cook for Mādhava, every hair on Your body stands erect in joy and Your gait falters. Will my eyes ever attain this vision?

Śrīmatī Rādhārāṇī, the most excellent and famous cook in all existence, because of the earnest entreaty of Yaśodā Mātā, daily goes to cook for Kṛṣṇa at Nanda-bhavana.

Once, Durvāsā Ṛṣi came to the palace in Varsānā and said, "Vṛṣabhānu Mahārāja, I am very hungry."

"I will quickly arrange whatever you like," Vṛṣabhānu Mahārāja said.

"I don't desire your cooking or the cooking of your wife. You are not pure. You share your life with everyone."

"Then what should I do?" "Do you have a daughter?" "Yes."

"Your daughter will cook."

"She is only a baby, how can She cook?"

"You are trying to cheat me. Call Her at once!"

Vṛṣabhānu Mahārāja brought Rādhārāṇī in his arms to Durvāsā Ṛṣi.

"O Lāḍlī," Durvāsā Ṛṣi asked, "I know You are an expert cook. All the demigods including Brahmā know of Your

special abilities and glorify Your super-excellent qualities. Won't You cook something for me?"

Rādhārānī smiled and said, "Yes."

"Please cook something quickly. I have not eaten for what seems like ages."

"What would you like?"

"I especially like *ksīra*," Durvāsā Ṛṣi replied, "and I also like *mālpuā* so much."

Śrīmatī Rādhārānī cooked sweet rice and *mālpuā*. She didn't make only one or two pieces of *mālpuā*. Durvāsā Ṛṣi doesn't eat one or two grams, a hundred grams, or even a hundred kilos. His appetite is immeasurable. Śrīmatī knew this. She cooked so much sweet rice, it was like the *kusuma-sarovara* lake, and She made so many *mālpuās*, they became a mountain like Girirāja Govardhana. How did She cook? All the *sakhīs* and *mañjarīs* are like Her expansions; they all know Her desire. They helped arrange everything. If Rādhārānī looks and touches anything, this is enough. So many things are arranged.

Durvāsā Ṛṣi sat down at eleven or twelve o'clock in the night and began eating. From midnight until early morning he ate, saying inbetween platefuls, "Bring more, bring more." He had more and more desire for this *mahā-prasāda*. He ate a plate, yawned, and then ate more, without taking any rest. By morning everything was finished. Then he said, "Now I am happy. Now I am satisfied."

His name is Durvāsā Ṛṣi. He checks if one has good or bad desires, *vāsāna*. If your desire is good, he will give you a passing certificate, otherwise if you have bad desires and moods, he will destroy you.

After eating, Durvāsā Ṛṣi gave a boon to Rādhikā: "This daughter of Vṛṣabhānu Mahārāja is *siddha*, perfect. Anything She touches becomes supremely auspicious and full of nectar. If anyone tastes Her cooking, or hears Her glories, remembers

Her, offers anything to Her, and then takes that, he will achieve love for God and *bhakti-rasa*. By once tasting that *rasa*, he will have no desire for other *rasas*. And if anyone is inimical to her, he will be destroyed."

In this verse, Dāsa Gosvāmī prays to accompany Śrīmatījī on Her way to Nanda-bhavana. All the *sakhīs* and *mañjarīs* walk with Śrīmatī Rādhārānī from Varsānā to Nandagrāma. Many *sakhīs* and *mañjarīs* come from different places in Vraja to meet with Śrīmatī Rādhārānī at Prema-sarovara, before proceeding to Nandagrāma. None of the *gopīs* come empty-handed. They bring many items, arranged at their homes for service in Rādhārānī's cooking.

pārśva-dvaye lalitayātha viśākhayā ca
tvāṁ sarvataḥ parijanaiś ca paraiḥ parītām
paścān mayā vibhṛta-bhaṅgura-madhya-bhāgaṁ
kiṁ rūpa-mañjarir iyaṁ pathi neṣyatīha
Vilāpa-kusumāñjali 59

When will Rūpa Mañjarī lead You on the path with Lalitā and Viśākhā at Your two sides, Your friends all around, and me holding Your delicate waist from behind?

On the way to Nandagrāma, Lalitā and Viśākhā walk alongside Rādhārānī. Here, Dāsa Gosvāmī prays to walk behind holding Śrīmatījī's waist. Rūpa Mañjarī walks in front with Rādhikā, while carrying many things. Absorbed in his internal form as Rati Mañjarī, Dāsa Gosvāmī sees Rūpa with a heavy load and thinks, "I will go forward and request Rūpa Mañjarī, 'Please give me something to carry.'" Rati Mañjarī doesn't want Rūpa Mañjarī to feel the slightest disturbance.

Kṛṣṇa understands everything. He is still resting in Nanda-bhavana, but by His desire, many bulls, camels, and elephants come to help bring paraphernalia from Varsānā to

Nanda-bhavana. They offer *praṇāma* to Śrīmatī Rādhārāṇī, bending down on their knees. The elephants clean the pathway with their tusks and sprinkle the road with flowers. Then the animals carry the items for cooking. The animals of Vraja also have service tendency and don't merely eat, sleep, and wander about, enjoying the love and affection of Kṛṣṇa. They have pure knowledge and service tendency.

hamvārair iha gavām api ballavānāṁ
kolāhalair vividha-vandi-kalāvatāṁ taiḥ
samrājate priyatayā vraja-rāja-sūnor
govardhanād api gurur vraja-vanditād yaḥ

prāptāṁ nija-praṇayinī-prakaraiḥ parītāṁ
nandīśvaraṁ vraja-mahendra-mahālayaṁ taṁ
dūre nirīkṣya muditā tvaritaṁ dhaniṣṭhā
tvām ānayiṣyati kadā praṇayair mamāgre

Vilāpa-kusumāñjali 60–61

Surrounded by Your affectionate *gopī* friends, You arrive at Nandiśvara, which is filled with the mowing of the cows, the shouts of the cowherders and the different songs of minstrels, and which is dearer to the prince of Vraja than even Govardhana. When will I then see Dhaniṣṭhā, who has seen you coming from afar, quickly and lovingly take You inside, as I follow behind You?

Nandiśvara Hill is extremely dear to Nanda-nandana. The Vrajavāsīs pray and offer respect to Girirāja Govardhana, but an even sweeter and important place is Nandiśvara Hill. Kṛṣṇa dearly loves Nandiśvara and always resides there. Kṛṣṇa sometimes go to Govardhana and performs pastimes there, accepting the service of Girirāja, but Nandiśvara is always able to serve Kṛṣṇa and His associates.

Dāsa Gosvāmī prays, "When will I go to Nandiśvara and pray to him for service. But only service is not enough. If I have no position there, my mind will be disturbed by *asat-sāṅga*."

Sat-saṅga doesn't only mean to stay with *sādhus* for some time and then go some place else. One must continuously stay with *sādhus*, with love for them, not by hook or crook. If I have a loving relation with the *sādhus*, they will give me a place to stay.

Dāsa Gosvāmī prays, "I will not stay for selfish purposes, nor will I try to acquire and possess any place. Any place I am present, I will keep it only for Śrīmatījī and the *sakhīs* and will endeavor to serve them there."

Dhanisṭhā is very dear to Śrīmatī Rādhārāṇī. She is her beloved *sakhī*. Mother Yaśodā gives her great respect. Dhaniṣṭhā serves in Nanda-bhavana, dividing all responsibilities so that everything can be accomplished properly.

Dāsa Gosvāmī prays, "When will Dhaniṣṭhā take me to Vrajeśvarī Yaśodā, and say, 'This Lālī has so much love for service.' "

On one side Lalitā is present, and Viśākhā is on the other side, but this Rati is waiting behind. Whenever Dhaniṣṭhā calls her forth, she does everything on her instruction.

At the time of *smaraṇa-daśā*, internally meditating on one's perfected state and form, and going near one's worshipable Kṛṣṇa, all Kṛṣṇa's associates are present there. They will instruct you, "This is your service. This is your place." There will be no need for any subtle hint or indication. One will understand which direction to go and how to serve. The path will be clear, without any obstacles. Don't think this is speculation or if you go there you won't know what to do, or how to engage your time. It is not like this. The flow of inspiration and mercy is very powerful. It will sweep you up.

Many people are in Russia, America, Africa, Australia, Europe, or India. When they meet Gurudeva and join his mission, at first they don't know what to do or what their service will be. But automatically, by Gurudeva's inspiration, they take their own places and responsibilities and perform their specific service very seriously. Gradually their taste for service will increase more and more and there will be no need for any permit, permission, advice, instruction, or company officer to give one duty and sign one in, checking if one is performing one's service properly and doing the proper amount of hours. This is only as an example. In the eternal world, there is a powerful force, inspiring one to serve.

prakṣālya pāda-kamale kuśale praviṣṭā
natvā vrajeśa-mahiṣī-prabhṛtīr gurūs taiḥ
hā kurvatī rasavatīṁ rasa-bhāk kadā tvaṁ
sammajayiṣyatitarāṁ sukha-sāgare mām

Vilāpa-kusumāñjali 62

O auspicious one, You are an expert cook. After I wash Your lotus feet, You enter the kitchen and offer Your obeisances to the queen of Vraja and the other elder *gopīs*. When will You plunge me into an ocean of bliss by doing this?

Dāsa Gosvāmī prays, "When will I wash the feet of Śrīmatījī and those of my seniors, like Nanda Mahārāja, Yaśodā Mātā, and others. I will offer them *praṇāma*, accept their blessings, and then go to cook in the kitchen. By their strength and mercy I will be a perfect assistant to Śrimātījī."

Yaśodā Mātā and Rohiṇī Mātā are expert cooks. Durvāsā Ṛṣi also came to Yaśodā Mātā and after accepting her cooking, gave her a boon and the name Yaśodā, saying, "Your *yaśa*, fame, will spread all over the world. Everyone will follow your order and advice. If anyone neglects you, he will lose his strength and life."

Therefore Yaśodā Mātā is famous and knows how to cook and arrange everything expertly.

How can one enter the flow of service and taste the nectar of Vraja? The *sādhaka's* first duty is to go to his elders and seniors—those who are perfected in their service. One should go to one's Guru-varga and offer them *praṇāma*, wash their feet, offer flowers and sandal paste at their lotus feet, and pray to them, "How can I be trained to perfectly serve? Please bless me with your love and potency."

There are thousands of fire pits in the kitchen. As Śrīmatījī cooks in a white dress, pearls of sweat form on Her golden limbs. Rati Mañjarī stands nearby with soft pieces of cotton, with which she dabs Śrīmatī's skin, removing the moisture so it doesn't fall in the cooking.

mādhavāya nata-vaktram ādṛtā
bhojya-peya-rasa-sañcayaṁ kramāt
tanvatī tvam iha rohiṇī-kare
devi phulla-vadanaṁ kadekṣyase

Vilāpa-kusumāñjali 63

O Devī, when can I see You, with Your head lowered and Your blushing face looking affectionately at Mādhava, as You collect all the ambrosial foods and drinks and place them in Rohiṇī-devī's hands?

In Nanda-bhavana, Rohiṇī-devī is senior and perfect at all things. She knows how to make drinks that attract Mādhava's mind and spark His appetite. He sometimes goes outside to play with His friends and will not return, becoming so absorbed in playing. Rohiṇī Mātā makes a wonderful drink and takes this outside, saying, "Kṛṣṇa, come, come."

But He will not come. When she went to catch Him, He ran away and would not come to her. Finally she catches Kṛṣṇa and gives Him the drink. Taking it, Kṛṣṇa becomes very hungry! Then He says, "Yes, yes, I will come with you."

Rohiṇī Mātā perfectly knows how to cook and distribute *prasāda*. It is not enough simply to cook nicely—the process of distribution must be learnt as well. The preparations must be served in the correct order. In some places, people go and give *rasagullas, halava*, and *mālpuā* first, and then give sweet drinks, and then the digestive fire is stopped and you can't stomach the main courses. When distributing *prasāda*, one first gives something bitter, like a *karela* dish. A small amount of something bitter at the beginning of the meal increases the appetite and digestive fire. Then you give rice, *dāl, pakoṛās, roti* or *puris* then a dry *sabji* and other *sabjis*, like *panir-sabji*, and then chutney and *pappadams*. After this you give yogurt, *rasagullas*, sweet rice, and other sweets. Then you give something salty and sweet. At the end, you give a lemon drink mixed with cumin powder. Otherwise, you give buttermilk with cumin seeds and black pepper, and then the meal will be easily digested. There is a proper process to do everything. But if you don't know anything, how can you serve in Vraja-maṇḍala?

In Nanda-bhavana, all the elders, like Nanda Mahārāja, his brothers, father, mother and other relatives sit down in line. Kṛṣṇa sits with Nanda Bābā. How can anything special be given just to Kṛṣṇa? Kṛṣṇa's expression is examined from a distance to see what He desires. Who understands this? Everything reflects into the kitchen room, where Rādhārāṇī is present. She then sends the proper preparations. But She doesn't come Herself. She sends Rati Mañjarī or any other *mañjarī*. She instructs, "Go and give this to Yaśodā Mātā. She will give it to Kṛṣṇa."

bhojane guru-sabhāsu kathañcin
mādhavena nata-dṛṣṭi-madotkam
vīkṣyamānam iha te mukha-padmaṁ
modayiṣyasi kadā madhure mām

Vilāpa-kusumāñjali 64

O sweet one, when will I see Your joyful and eager lotus face, as Your passionate sidelong glances are seen by Mādhava, while He feasts in the company of His elders?

Dāsa Gosvāmī now prays to see the lotus face of Śrīmatī as She cooks and castes sidelong glances at Kṛṣṇa. Dāsa Gosvāmī, in his eternal form as Rati Mañjari, assists Śrīmatī Rādhārāṇī while She cooks. She places all the paraphernalia close to Śrīmatī with great care. She doesn't serve out of duty or on any condition. Everything she does is performed out of her heartfelt love. As she serves, her body sweats and undergoes ecstatic symptoms. Śrīmatī Rādhārāṇī, Kṛṣṇa, Vrajapati Nanda Mahārāja, and Yaśodā Mātā are very pleased with her.

Kṛṣṇa follows proper etiquette while taking *prasāda*. He shows by example how juniors should lovingly serve and show respect to their elders. First they distribute the *praśāda* to all the elders. Then on the elders' request, the juniors also take.

While eating, beads of perspiration appear on Kṛṣṇa's body. The *mañjarīs* immediately begin to fan Him. Nanda Mahārāja is present there. He says, "Oh, you small *kiśorīs* will become exhausted. Don't exert yourselves so much." Yet Rūpa Mañjarī and Rati Mañjarī continue to fan, as Nanda Bābā feeds *prasāda* to Kṛṣṇa and Baladeva, with one on each side of him. Rati Mañjarī watches Kṛṣṇa's expression while He eats and reports His reactions to the different items. The *mañjarīs* serve second helpings of whatever He likes. It is not that they give everything at once; rather, they bring fresh, hot *rotis* and *pūrīs*, one at a time, along with other preparations, and then watch from afar how Kṛṣṇa reacts to the different dishes.

There are many mothers who serve Kṛṣṇa with *vātsalya-rasa*, not only Yaśodā. The mothers request the *mañjarīs* to help serve out *prasādam*. Lalitā and the other *sakhīs* are shy there. They do not go near Kṛṣṇa while He eats. And Kṛṣṇa doesn't say what He likes. He is silent and takes whatever comes. Even if He desires more of something in particular, He doesn't mention it to anyone.

From the kitchen, Yaśodā Mātā says, "O Rati, go and give Kṛṣṇa this." Rati Mañjarī is only three or four years old. Sometimes Yaśodā Mātā says to her, "Ask Kṛṣṇa what He likes. Go sit close to Him and ask Him what He likes most, and He will tell you. Otherwise, just observe what He is eating with extra enthusiasm, then come tell me and I will send more of that."

The *sakhīs* want to do this, but they are too shy to go forward in front of Nanda Bābā and all the elders of Vraja.

Yaśodā Mātā is not the only mother with deep love for Kṛṣṇa. Kṛṣṇa's aunts and all the mothers of Vraja love Him dearly.

Yaśodā Mātā strokes Rati and tells her, "Go and check what He likes. Also ask Baladeva, Sudāma, Śrīdāma, Stoka-kṛṣṇa, Mahārāja Parjanya, and the others in line what they would like."

Otherwise some doubt may come, "Why does Rati Mañjarī give Kṛṣṇa particular attention?"

Rati Mañjarī goes and asks Sudāma and Śrīdāma, "What would you like? Do you want another *pappadam* or some chutney?"

Śrīdāma says, "Yes, bring chutney!"

Then Rati brings some chutney and *pakoṛās*.

The *sakhās* are also very clever. They don't express their own desire. They sit beside Kṛṣṇa and can tell what He would like more of. They indicate in a secret way or whisper very quietly, "Oh, bring this preparation quickly. It is very nice."

Rati brings it and comes to give some to Sudāma, but he says, "No, I don't like this. Put it on Kṛṣṇa's plate." The *sakhās* understand Kṛṣṇa's desire and give indications to the *mañjarīs*.

12

Caraṇa Sevā

ayi vipinam aṭantaṁ saurabheyī-kulānāṁ
vraja-nṛpati-kumāraṁ rakṣaṇe dīkṣitaṁ tam
vikala-mati-jananyā lālyamānaṁ kadā tvaṁ
smita-madhura-kapolaṁ vīkṣyase vīkṣyamānā

Vilāpa-kusumāñjali 65

When will I see You gazing upon the prince of Vraja, His cheeks sweetened with a smile, as His mother anxiously strokes Him while He departs for the forest, fulfilling His vow to protect the *surabhi* cows?

Dāsa Gosvāmī now prays to be near Rādhārāṇī as She watches Kṛṣṇa passing by on His way to go grazing the cows, when mother Yaśodā embraces him. For the service and protection of the noble members of the *surabhi* dynasty of cows, Kṛṣṇa daily enters the forests of Vraja. Kṛṣṇa took a vow to always serve the cows. He does not go to the same place every day, in consideration of the area, not wanting to overburden it with all the cows.

Mother Yaśodā worries about Kṛṣṇa, thinking, "Gopāla is only a small boy, but He daily goes out in the summer heat or winter chill, despite rain or any other harsh weather; He never takes rest. The sun is strong and burns Him. How can I protect Him?" She has affectionate concern for Kṛṣṇa's welfare.

Kṛṣṇa's earrings kiss His cheeks. He smiles and looks side to side. Yaśodā Mātā watches His every movement. She thinks, "What is helpful for Kṛṣṇa?" and she is ready to arrange anything at once. Kṛṣṇa has relation and love for anyone who resides in Gokula and promises to protect and serve all those who come and stay in Vraja. This relation is not any ordinary

or temporary thing. Kṛṣṇa does not make friendship with anyone for a day; His love is eternal.

Kṛṣṇa is the prince of Vraja, but He doesn't consider Himself royalty too superior to serve. He does not feel that He is a highly respectable authority. This is not His nature.

Vṛndāvana has many forests. When Kṛṣṇa takes the cows out to graze, He is not only taking care of the cows, but He takes care of the forests and gardens as well. The creepers, plants, and trees will become dry if they are not taken care of. The cows trim the grass and keep it clean and healthy.

Farmers clean and till their fields to keep them fertile and healthy. The cows are like the gardeners of Vraja, keeping everything fresh and pure by fertilizing the forests and aerating the land. The cow dung and urine make those areas healthy and vibrant. This is food for the plants and trees. If the cows did not graze in the forests, then the greenery would not get this extra nourishment. In the forest, there are many varieties of plants and medicinal herbs. By eating these plants and herbs, the cows' udders become filled with wholesome milk. In this way, everyone benefits by Kṛṣṇa taking the cows out to graze. Therefore Kṛṣṇa vows to always care for the cows, Vrajavāsīs, and forests of Vraja.

As Kṛṣṇa goes through the forests, He accepts the trees and plants' heartfelt gifts of fruits and flowers and distributes them to the *sakhās*.

Yaśodā Mātā is always concerned for Kṛṣṇa's welfare when He is in the forests of Vraja. To pacify her, Rati Mañjarī says, "O Nandarānī, don't worry. I will go to the forest and look after Kṛṣṇa. I will change my appearance and will help arrange for Kṛṣṇa's service while He is grazing the cows. Rādhikā will also cook some refreshments for Kṛṣṇa. I will help arrange all this. The *mañjarīs* and I are ready to see that Kṛṣṇa is cared for while He is outside Nanda-bhavana."

Yaśodā Mātā is pleased to hear this and says, "Oh! You will take care of my Kanhaiyā? He cares for everyone, but I always worry about who will take care of Him." Yaśodā Mātā is very happy to hear that the *sakhīs* and *mañjarīs* are there to help Kṛṣṇa in the forest and she gives her blessings to Rati Mañjarī.

goṣṭheśayātha kutukāc chapathādi-pūrvaṁ
su-snigdhayā sumukhi mātṛ-parārdhato 'pi
hā hrī-mati priya-gaṇaiḥ saha bhojyamānāṁ
kiṁ tvāṁ nirīkṣya hṛdaye mudam adya lāpsye
Vilāpa-kusumāñjali 66

O bashful fair-faced one! When will my heart feel great joy to see the queen of Vraja, who is more affectionate than countless mothers, taking an oath to make You sit down to eat with Your friends?

Dāsa Gosvāmī in his internal form as Rati Mañjarī prays to Rādhārāṇī, "O Śrīmatī, You are supremely beautiful. Seeing You, people become filled with joy, and in the absence of Your *darśana* everyone becomes distressed. In Nanda-bhavana, while eating, without Your *darśana* the food has no taste for Kṛṣṇa."

After Kṛṣṇa finishes His meal, Yaśoda Mātā affectionately requests Śrīmatī to take prasāda. Rādhārāṇī becomes shy. She sits down with Lalitā, Viśākhā, and the other *sakhīs* and takes something. Rati Mañjarī feels great bliss observing Śrīmatījī as She tastes Her cooking. As Kṛṣṇa ate, Śrīmatī watched from a hidden place, and Kṛṣṇa would casually look up now and again and They exchanged sidelong glances. Now, when Rādhārāṇī sits to eat on the request of Yaśodā Mātā, Kṛṣṇa comes and peeks through the window to watch His beloved. Receiving *darśana* of Śrīmatī is Kṛṣṇa's favorite nourishment.

While Kṛṣṇa eats, Śrīmatī watches from a hidden place and waits for Him to finish. When Kṛṣṇa gets up and leaves, as the elders and other guests in Nanda-bhavana are otherwise preoccupied, He and Śrīmatī look for a chance to momentarily meet. Śrīmatī wants to meet with Kṛṣṇa and begins walking away from the kitchen, but then Yaśodā Mātā calls out to Her, "O Lālī, come eat something."

Rādhārānī returns unwillingly and sits down to eat. In the meantime, Kṛṣṇa waits at the secret meeting place for Śrīmatī. When She doesn't arrive, Kṛṣṇa comes to where She is eating with Yaśodā and Her *sakhīs*. On the pretense of asking Yaśodā something, He glances lovingly at Śrīmatī from the corner of His eyes. Rādhārānī blushes and covers Her face with a cloth while She takes *prasāda* with the *sakhīs* and Yaśodā. Seeing this in his meditation, Dāsa Gosvāmī becomes overjoyed.

āliṅganena śirasaḥ paricumbanena
snehāvalokana-bhareṇa ca khañjanākṣi
goṣṭheśayā nava-vadhūm iva lālyamānām
tvāṁ prekṣya kiṁ hṛdi mahotsavam ātaniṣye
Vilāpa-kusumāñjali 67

O Rādhe, eyes restless as *khañjana* birds! When will I experience a festival of joy seeing You being fondled by the queen of Vraja, who embraces You, kisses Your head, and gazes upon You lovingly as if You were Her newly married daughter-in-law?

Like a newly married girl who comes to serve at the house of her husband after marriage, Śrīmatī Rādhārānī comes in the early morning to Nandagrāma with Her *sakhīs* and *mañjarīs* to cook for Kṛṣṇa.

While Rādhārānī is still on the pathway to Nandagrāma, Yaśodā Mātā comes down to meet Her. She runs and embraces Śrīmatī Rādhārānī. She smells Her head, kisses Her, lifts Her into her arms, and carries Her up the hill to her own room.

There she gives Śrīmatī Rādhārāṇī new earrings, necklaces, *saris*, and many other gifts. She gives Her so many new things every day. She embraces and kisses each of the young girls and gives them many gifts.

Why does Yaśodā Mātā have this heartfelt love for them all? If anyone desires to serve Kṛṣṇa, then Yaśodā is very pleased and has so much love for that person. She serves and thinks of everyone's welfare.

Dāsa Gosvāmī prays, "When will I be present in Nanda-bhavana, and under guidance of Yaśodā Mātā, I will assist Śrīmatī Rādhārāṇī in the kitchen. Love and affection will flow from Yaśodā Mātā's heart to all the *sakhīs* and *mañjarīs*."

Anything done with love is very sweet. Kṛṣṇa longs for that love. Śrīmatī Rādhārāṇī's *hlādinī-śakti* spreads out to the hearts of all the Vrajavāsīs, like a transcendental sun of love, and shines in the hearts of those in the moods of *dāsya-rasa*, *sakhya-rasa*, *vātsalya-rasa*, and *mādhurya-rasa*.

hā rūpa-mañjari sakhi praṇayena devīṁ
tvad-bāhu-datta-bhuja-vallarim āyatākṣīm
paścād ahaṁ kalita-kāma-taraṅga-raṅgāṁ
neṣyāmi kiṁ hari-vibhūṣita-keli-kuñjam

Vilāpa-kusumāñjali 68

O dear friend Rūpa Mañjarī, when will I, from behind, lead our Devī, who has become a dancing arena for waves of amorous passion, Her large eyes wide-open, and Your arm affectionately placed about the vine of Her waist, to the *keli-kuñja* forest grove, decorated by the presence of Śrī Hari?

Dāsa Gosvāmī prays to accompany Śrīmatī as She goes to the *keli-kuñja*. In his internal form as Rati Mañjarī, Dāsa Gosvāmī is there, watching Kṛṣṇa's playful pastimes. Rati Mañjarī is present behind Rūpa Mañjarī and they walk with Śrīmatī to the *keli-kuñja*. Rūpa Mañjarī has decorated the *kuñja*, making a brilliant throne of flowers. Śrīmatī Rādhārāṇī sits on the flower throne in the *kuñja* and eagerly awaits Kṛṣṇa's arrival.

If there is no sweet relation, then no one will want to follow behind another. Ordinarily, people follow others for their own selfishness, but this temporary relationship is contemptible, whereas the sweet relation between the Vrajavāsīs is most glorious.

Rati Mañjarī thinks, "When will I carry Kṛṣṇa's loving presentations and give them to Rūpa Mañjarī?"

Rūpa Mañjarī will not accept anything independently. She offers anything that comes to her to Śrīmatī Rādhārāṇī. Kṛṣṇa sends a necklace or a beautiful garland to Rūpa Mañjarī through the hand of Rati Mañjarī. Rati Mañjarī shows this gift to Śrīmatī Rādhārāṇī, then Rādhārāṇī gives it to Rūpa Mañjarī, and says, "No, no. This is good for you, you should accept it."

This garland isn't only made of flowers. Kṛṣṇa's heartfelt love is contained within. After much opposition, Rūpa Mañjarī wears this *mālā* by Rādhārāṇī's insistance; she becomes very shy and looks down, experiencing Kṛṣṇa's love present in this gift.

sākaṁ tvayā sakhi nikuñja-gṛhe sarasyāḥ
svasyās taṭe kusuma-bhāvita-bhuṣaṇena
śṛṅgāritaṁ vidadhatī priyam īśvarī sā
hā hā bhaviṣyati mad-īkṣaṇa-gocaraḥ kim

Vilāpa-kusumāñjali 69

My dear friend Rūpa Mañjarī, when will I be able to see you with my mistress decorating Her beloved with flower ornaments in a *kuñja-kuṭīra* by the bank of Her lake?

Śrīmatī Rādhikā is in an isolated grove on the bank of Rādhā-kuṇḍa. Rūpa is nearby, feeling that although the *kuñja-kuṭīra* is decorated with beautiful flowers, it is lacking perfect beauty because Kṛṣṇa is not there. Rūpa Mañjarī finds some means to invite Kṛṣṇa, who comes and sits on a seat of flowers. The *sakhīs* begin to fan Him. The flowers are fragrant, but Kṛṣṇa is restless. The flowers and fans do not cool Him. He is unsatisfied. Why?

Kṛṣṇa says, "O Rūpa Mañjarī, when will your *adhīśvari* Śrīmatī Rādhārāṇī give Me *darśana*? I came here only for Her *darśana*."

Rūpa Mañjarī replies, "My Svāminī is resting inside a *kuñja* nearby." "I came only for Her *darśana*," Kṛṣṇa repeats.

Rūpa Mañjarī gives an indication to Rati Mañjarī, who goes and tells Rādhārāṇī. Hearing Kṛṣṇa's message, Śrīmatī Rādhārāṇī hides deeper in the *kuñja-kuṭīra*, not wanting to give Him *darśana* so easily. When Rati returns, Kṛṣṇa begins to search for Rādhikā.

śrutvā vicakṣaṇa-mukhād vraja-rāja-sūnoḥ
śastābhisāra-samayaṁ subhage 'tra hṛṣṭā
sūkṣmāmbaraiḥ kusuma-saṁskṛta-karṇa-pūra-
hārādibhiś ca bhavatīṁ kim alaṅkariṣye

Vilāpa-kusumāñjali 70

O beautiful one, hearing from the parrot Vicakṣaṇa that the prince of Vraja has already left for His rendezvous with You, can I joyfully decorate You with fine garments, flower earrings, and necklaces?

In Vraja, there is a clever parrot named Vicakṣaṇa, who witnesses Rādhā-Kṛṣṇa's sweet loving pastimes and repeats them to the *gopīs*. Sometimes this parrot brings messages back and forth between Rādhārāṇī's camp and Kṛṣṇa's camp.

Once, Kṛṣṇa sent Vicakṣaṇa on an errand, saying, "Go and search out where there are nice flowers. Collect them and give them to Me. I will make flower earrings and will decorate a dress and make many flower ornaments for Rādhārānī. Then I will take these and present them to Her." This parrot returns sometime later and says to Nanda-nandana, "I went to search for flowers and found the Vraja-devīs making a dress for You embroidered with flowers. They want to give You flower earrings, ornaments, and flowers."

Kṛṣṇa replies, "I will decorate and serve them."

"If You first accept their loving presentations," Vicakṣaṇa replies, "then You will realize how they will be pleased and will be able to serve them in return."

Kṛṣṇa's desires reflect in Rādhārānī's heart and She instructs Her *mañjarīs* how to fulfill those desires. They then make new outfits with silk, pearls, flowers, and jewels. When Kṛṣṇa wears these clothes, He feels that Śrīmatī Rādhārānī is directly present with Him. Śrīmatī Rādhārānī's love and the love of the *sakhīs* and *mañjarīs* is present in whatever they touch.

nānā-puṣpaiḥ kvanita-madhupair devi sambhāvitābhir
mālābhis tad-ghusṛṇa-vilasat-kāma-citrālibhiś ca
rājad-dvāre sapadi madanānandadābhikhya-gehe
malli-jālaiḥ śaśi-mukhi kadā talpam ākalpayāmi

Vilāpa-kusumāñjali 71

O moon-faced one, when will I arrange a bed of jasmine flowers for You in Madanānandada-kuñja, which has a beautiful gate and is decorated with wonderful pictures of Cupid, drawn in *kuṁkum*, and garlands of many flowers, surrounded by buzzing bees.

The glories of this Madanānanda-kuñja are explained herein. It is located near Pāvana-sarovara, not far from Nanda-bhavana. Kṛṣṇa goes alone to that *kuñja* after waking in the morning, and rests for awhile in the arms of Śrīmatī and the Vraja-devīs.

Dāsa Gosvāmī prays, "O Devī, sweetly singing bumblebees move flower to flower, collecting honey. Hearing their singing, You open the door of the *kuñja* and look out expectantly, hoping for Kṛṣṇa to appear at any moment. I will decorate the doorway of that *kuñja* with draping strands of flowers and will arrange a bed in that forest grove for Your pleasure."

In the morning, the *sakhīs* and *mañjarīs* come with honey, drinks, flowers, and many offerings to cook with Rādhārāṇī at Nanda-bhavana. From a distance, Citrā-devī, who is most expert at making paintings, shows Śrīmatī Rādhārāṇī with her enchanting art where Kṛṣṇa is and what He is doing. Then Śrīmatī Rādhārāṇī arranges for His service.

Kṛṣṇa gets up in the morning, having stayed awake the whole night and therefore needing more rest. There is a special *kuñja-kuṭīra* arranged for Him to hide in and continue resting after He formally wakes in Nanda-bhavana.

He comes there by a hidden path. He disappears from the cowshed where He was milking the cows and enters this *kuñja*. Rādhārāṇī and the Vraja-devīs take Him in their arms. They massage Him and fan Him, and He interacts with each of them personally, resting His head on the knee of one, holding hands with another, and placing His arm around the shoulders of another. The hearts and bodies of the Vraja-devīs are more soft, delicate, beautiful and lovely than any flower. Each *gopī* makes her lap like a bed for Kṛṣṇa to rest on. Kṛṣṇa rests in Madanānandada-kuñja in the morning.

śrī-rūpa-mañjari-karārcita-pāda-padma-
goṣṭhendra-nandana-bhujārpita-mastakāyāḥ
hā modataḥ kanaka-gauri padāravinda-
saṁvāhanāni śanakais tava kiṁ kariṣye

Vilāpa-kusumāñjali 72

O golden one, when will I happily and gently massage Your lotus feet, along with Rūpa Mañjarī, as You rest Your head in the lap of the prince of Vraja, and He massages Your head?

Śrīmatī Rādhārānī comes from Varsānā and rests with Kṛṣṇa in Madanānanda-kuñja. She lies down, and Rūpa Mañjarī massages Her feet and soothes them with cool *kuṅkuma* and *mehindi.* As Rūpa Mañjarī serves the feet of Śrīmatī Rādhārānī, she signals to Rati Mañjarī to come forward and massage as well.

Sometimes, if He has permission, Kṛṣṇa sits with Śrīmatī Rādhārānī in His lap and as She rests on His knee, He strokes Her head. Rūpa Mañjarī massages the feet of the Divine Couple with her soft pleasing hands and calls Rati Mañjarī forward to assist her.

Dāsa Gosvāmī prays, "When will Rūpa Mañjarī call me forward for the service of Rādhā-Kṛṣṇa?"

The name 'Rūpa Mañjarī' means that with her beauty, she conquers and controls the hearts of all. There is no darkness in her heart. She is always bright, light, and golden.

Dāsa Gosvāmī prays, "When will that day come when, after serving Śrīmatī Rādhārānī and Śrī Kṛṣṇa, I will be able to serve Rūpa Mañjarī herself? When will she give me permission for this? How else will I receive proper training?"

govardhanādri-nikaṭe mukuṭena narma-
līlā-vidagdha-śirasāṁ madhusūdanena
dāna-cchalena bhavatīm avarudhyamānāṁ
drakṣyāmi kiṁ bhru-kuṭi-darpita-netra-yugmām
Vilāpa-kusumāñjali 73

When will I see You, Your eyebrows knitted and Your eyes burning with pride, as Madhusūdana, the crown on the heads of expert jesters, stops You near Govardhana Hill on the pretext of collecting a toll?

Kṛṣṇa comes with His *sakhās* to the foot of Govardhana and takes tax from the Vraja-devīs. He demands, "Give Me tax!

Then He says, "Actually, I am not a tax collector. I don't take anything by force. That is not right. It is not sweet for Me. Please give Me some charity."

Then a bit later He says, "No, no, charity is also not good. I am not a poor person or a beggar. Please give Me *dāna*, donation. By giving *dāna*, you yourselves will be benefited and become happy. If you give anything happily, the benefit will multiply ten times. Therefore, give Me *dāna*. If you don't give Me *dāna*, you will become a poor, dirty, narrow-minded beggar. I am great. Everyone knows this. Therefore if you give Me a donation, then My own greatness will come to you, and your hearts will be clean. You will become fair, fresh, and full of goodness. I am a qualified person. If you give *dāna* to bad people, they will make you dirty and contaminated. You will suffer life after life. But by giving a donation to those who are qualified, it is very good for you. The best thing to offer is yourself, so if you offer yourself as a donation to a person with all good qualities, it is best."

With these words, Kṛṣṇa tries to capture Śrīmatī Rādhārāṇī. He says, "Give everything to Me. Then I will accept and help you. If you don't give yourselves to Me, then you will be forced to give yourselves to cheaters. They don't have any strength to help you. Anything you have should be given to Me. I am a qualified and very powerful person."

With such clever words, Kṛṣṇa attempts to take everything the *gopīs* possess as *dāna*. He is not interested in anything small. With His crooked eyes, He scans for any particle of love, and is not happy until He receives every last drop.

Dāsa Gosvāmī prays, "I long to watch Kṛṣṇa's sweet playful pastimes with the Vraja-devīs."

Kṛṣṇa captures the *gopis*, heart and soul. Demigods and the incarnations of God do not take the *jīva's anarthas* away. They take respect and worship from the living entities, but they do not take everything. Kṛṣṇa, on the other hand, takes everything from the living entities. He purifies their hearts and in the place of what He has stolen, He plants the tendency to lovingly serve Him forever.

Girirāja Govardhana is very clever. He serves Rādhā-Kṛṣṇa's sweet intimate pastimes and also, by Kṛṣṇa's desire, he serves all the Vrajavāsīs and gives them the chance to serve Kṛṣṇa.

Girirāja Govardhana has no independent desire, no desire for any thanks from the Vrajavāsīs or Kṛṣṇa, nor any aspiration for name and fame. He doesn't expect others to come and extol his glories and qualities.

This is a problem for *sevakas*. If one is able to do *guru-sevā* and God's service, then this is the greatest chance available in one's life. God and Śrī Guru's acceptance of our service is their great mercy upon us. They are so kind to give us this opportunity. But there are those who after such service become very proud. Where does this false ego come from? A victim of its attack thinks, "Without me, this service could not be accomplished. What would Śrī Guru do without me?"

Performing *parikramā* of Girirāja is the way to make friendship with him. A sincere person will come to him, offer *pūjā* and *bhoga* and perform *parikramā*. To such a person, Girirāja Govardhana teaches everything about Kṛṣṇa's love and love for Kṛṣṇa. He gives this gift to those who make friendship with him, and he makes them strong and faithful. Then they will never go far away from Vraja-maṇḍala, and desire will never come to serve anyone other than Kṛṣṇa and the Vrajavāsīs.

13

The Lake and Her Mercy

tava tanu-vara-gandhāsaṅgi-vātena candrā-
vali-kara-kṛta-mallī-keli-talpāc cchalena
madhura-mukhi mukundaṁ kuṇḍa-tīre milantaṁ
madhupam iva kadāhaṁ vīkṣya darpaṁ kariṣye
Vilāpa-kusumāñjali 74

O sweet-faced one, when the breeze carries Your excellent fragrance to where Mukunda enjoys with Candrāvalī on the jasmine pastime-bed that she fashioned with her own hand, He finds a clever excuse to suddenly leave, and like a bumblebee leaving an inferior flower, comes to meet with You on the shore of Your lake. When will I proudly witness this?

Girirāja Govardhana has wonderful lakes, *kuṇḍas, kuñja-kuṭīras,* gardens, waterfalls, fruits, and flowers. The *gopīs* bathe in the lakes around Govardhana, and collect fruits and flowers from places such as Kusuma-sarovara, Mānasi-gaṅgā, Govinda-kuṇḍa, Rāsa-sthalī, and Kadamba-kandi. If one goes to these places, simply sitting there, one will be profoundly affected. Śrīmatī Rādhārāṇī and Kṛṣṇa are engaged in transcendental loving exchanges nearby, and the air accepts Their scent and distributes that supremely potent nectar. If anyone breathes in that air, then his nature will completely change. He will become intoxicated, maddened with love, and will forget where he came from and who he is. He loses his former nature, and he will take complete shelter of Girirāja Govardhana. He will become restless and greedy for more and more *kṛṣṇa-sevā* at every moment.

When a greedy bee smells the scent of honey, he begins to fly around in search of its source. He hunts the flower from which this sweet smell is emanating. Similarly, Śrīmatī Rādhārānī is present on the slope of Girirāja Govardhana. If a *sādhaka* comes in touch with Her fragrance his life changes.

He becomes very greedy for Mukunda's *darśana*. A deep eagerness comes in his heart, "Where is *rasika-śekhara* Kṛṣṇa?"

Kṛṣṇa plays His flute everywhere around Girirāja Govardhana, and He meets with the Vraja-devīs in Govardhana's *kuñjas*. Sometimes He goes to Candra-sarovara, to the *kuñja* of Candrāvalī. There she offers Him a garland of *mallikā* flowers.

Later, Kṛṣṇa comes to Rādhā-kuṇḍa, still wearing that garland. But He sees that no one talks with Him, meets with Him, or even looks at Him. He then feels dry and despondent.

"Oh, this garland is very wicked," He says in disgust and casts aside the gift from Candrāvalī. He then bathes in Śyāma-kuṇḍa and Rādhā-kuṇḍa, and feels a little better. He then comes before the *gopīs* and prays at their feet for mercy and for Rādhārānī's *darśana*. Feeling a breeze that has touched Rādhārānī and come to Him, He experiences great bliss and His heart is cooled.

In his *Rādhā-rasa-sudhā-nidhi*, Śrīla Prabhodānanda Sarasvatī glorifies Śrīmatī Rādhārānī as follows:

yasyāḥ kadāpī vasanāṣcala-khelanottha-
dhanyāti-dhanya-pavanena kṛtārtha-mānī
yogīndra-durgama-gatir madhusūdano 'pi
tasyā namo 'stu vṛṣabhānu-bhuvo diśe 'pi

Rādhā-rasa-sudhā-nidhi 2

Obeisances to the direction that faces Śrī Vṛṣabhānu's daughter. When the breeze, coming from that direction, playfully moves the edge of Her garment, Madhusūdana, who cannot be attained by even the greatest *yogīs*, thinks that His life has become a great success.

By some sly process, Candrāvalī's followers brought Kṛṣṇa to their *kuñja*. There they offered Kṛṣṇa a nice outfit and decorated Him. He thought, "If I go like this to Rādhā-kuṇḍa everyone will be pleased with Me." But when He reached Rādhā-kuṇḍa He found that no one was pleased at all. It seemed that even Girirāja Govardhana neglected Him. Why? Girirāja is Śrīmatī Rādhārāṇī's follower. Therefore he also ignored Kṛṣṇa. Every *kuṇḍa* and *kuñja-kuṭīra* at Govardhana is cold to Kṛṣṇa and Kṛṣṇa cannot find anyone there, not even any animals.

He looked around and thought, "I must have done something quite wrong."

He looked down at His outfit and became saddened. "Because of these garments Rādhārāṇī's *gopīs* have become angry and have hidden from Me? Where have they gone?" Then He prays deeply.

Suddenly, from the north side of Rādhā-kuṇḍa, where Śrīmatī Rādhārāṇī is sitting with the *sakhīs*, a breeze touches Śrīmatī Rādhārāṇī's lotus feet and takes their fragrant message to the south side of Rādhā-kuṇḍa, where Kṛṣṇa is present. When Kṛṣṇa smells this, He comes to His senses.

"This attire is not good for Me," He thinks, and He takes off His outfit and ornaments. He purifies Himself by bathing in Śyāma-kuṇḍa and Rādhā-kuṇḍa. "Yes," He says, "now I'm feeling better."

Then He sees some *mañjarīs* have approached. "Your body has a horrible smell," they say, "clearly You have gone to the abode of many buffaloes. Perhaps You didn't herd cows today and played with buffaloes instead. Has Brahmā come and stolen Your cows again? Has Viśvāmṛta given You buffaloes to herd in their place? Buffaloes are very dirty; they like to sleep in drains and bathe in foul water. But cows are always neat and clean. You have definitely been with buffaloes, for Your body has such a foul scent."

The *mañjarīs* bring *candana, sugandhi, arbaṭa*, and other fragrant substances and ask Kṛṣṇa, "Shall we clean You?"

"This will not do," Kṛṣṇa says, "only the dust of Vraja will suffice."

"Yes, Rādhārānī's footdust will purify You," the *manjarīs* respond. "You should beware of the other side. Your desire and nature will change if You go to the other side. If You interact with Candrāvalī's party then Rādhika's group will shun You."

"I was not happy with Candrāvalī," Kṛṣṇa said, "so I came to drink the sweet honey of Rādhārānī's affection. I left Candrāvalī and came to Rādhā-kuṇḍa and cleansed Myself in the pure nectar of the water that bathed Śrīmatījī. Now will She accept me?"

samastād unmatta-bhramara-kula-jhaṅkāra-nikarair
lasat-padma-stomair api vihaga-rāvair api param
sakhī-vṛndaiḥ svīyaiḥ sarasi madhure prāṇa-patinā
kadā drakṣyāmas te śaśi-mukhi navaṁ keli-nivaham
Vilāpa-kusumāñjali 75

O sweet, moon-faced one, when will I witness Your ever-fresh water-sports with the Lord of Your heart and Your friends in Your sweet lake, which is filled with a host of splendid lotuses and is surrounded by chirping birds and humming bees?

Śrīmatī Rādhārānī is present at Rādhā-kuṇḍa, where atop splendid lotuses, there are many honeybees that hum sweetly and feast on nectar.

There are also many birds in all directions that sing happily. Why are they so happy? Receiving Your *darśana*, the hearts of the *sakhīs*, *mañjarīs*, birds, and animals are filled with happiness."

Kṛṣṇa has left Candrāvalī's *kuñja* and Śrīmatī Rādhārāṇī's victory is celebrated in bliss. The *sakhīs* sing, dance, and joke with Kṛṣṇa. Everyone waits for that *darśana*. How is that *rasa*? It is like when the full moon rises and everyone becomes naturally joyful. Kṛṣṇa, the lord of the Vraja-devīs' hearts, has come and now the *gopīs* celebrate. There is a great assembly of birds singing. Bees are drinking nectar amidst the swirls of fragrant lotuses and their buzzing adds to the birds' musical performance.

Dāsa Gosvāmī prays to be present during that occasion, waiting to see what happens next. He is ready, "What orders will come to me? I will arrange everything needed. When inspiration comes, I will quickly perform my service for Rādhārāṇī."

This wonderful program on the bank of Rādhā-kuṇḍa starts in the morning. There are many types of flowers in the *kuñja-kuṭīras* surrounding Rādhā-kuṇḍa, and an ocean of bliss pervades the whole atmosphere. The *sakhīs* and *mañjarīs* are very busy there, decorating the *kuñjas*.

When will that Rādhā-kuṇḍa give us Rādhikā's *darśana* and admission into eternal service? Dāsa Gosvāmī says, "Without the mercy of Rādhā-kuṇḍa one will not be able to enter the camp of Rādhārāṇī and follow Her footsteps, nor will one understand the secrets of Kṛṣṇa's service."

Rādhā-kuṇḍa is the place in Vraja-maṇḍala where all favorable things are present for Śrīmatī Rādhārāṇī's service.

sarovara-lasat-taṭe madhupa-guñji-kuñjāntare
sphuṭat-kusuma-saṅkule vividha-puṣpa-saṅghair mudā
ariṣṭa-jayinā kadā tava varoru bhūṣā-vidhīr
vidhāsyata iha priyaṁ mama sukhābdhim ātanvatā

Vilāpa-kusumāñjali 76

> O beautiful-thighed one, when will the ocean of my bliss expand to see Kṛṣṇa, the victor over Ariṣṭāsura, happily decorate You with many kinds of flowers in a *kuñja*, filled with blossoming flowers and humming bees, on the splendid bank of Your lake?

In Rādhā-kuṇḍa, if anything contrary enters, Kṛṣṇa destroys it. Like when Ariṣṭāsura came to Vraja, Kṛṣṇa destroyed him. What does this mean? If a person comes to Rādhā-kuṇḍa and sits on Her bank, at the lotus feet of Rādhārānī, then any *ariṣṭa*, demonic mundane desire, will not be able to come and cheat that *sādhaka*, pulling him away from service to Śrīmatījī. Kṛṣṇa is present there with a strong mood, ready to destroy any opposition. Any *anarthas* or unwanted desires will be unable to disturb one. The *sādhaka* will have no further troubles. Kṛṣṇa will give him a sweet nature and good desires.

At Rādhā-kuṇḍa, the *sakhīs* are busy serving Rādhārāṇī. Some are painting designs on Her hands and feet, and some are combing Her hair, which they decorate with small flowers.

The *mañjarīs* say, "Collect peacock feathers here. Kṛṣṇa likes them so much." Then they collect peacock feathers and make crowns with them and give these to the *sakhīs*. Then they make dresses. After Kṛṣṇa bathes, they will decorate and dress Him. The *sakhīs* and *mañjarīs* are ready to perform this service.

On the other side, the *sādhakas* see that the *gopīs* are busily engaged in serving Śrīmatī Rādhārāṇī. Kṛṣṇa has come Himself and is waiting for a chance to serve Rādhārāṇī. He prays to the *sakhīs* and *mañjarīs*, "When will you give Me chance to comb Rādhārāṇī's hair? I will separate Her hairs and will gently braid them. How will I make a sweet relation with Her hair? I will massage oil into Her hair, made fragrant with *kastūrī*, and then I will place flowers and pollen in Her charming locks."

Kṛṣṇa prays to the *gopīs* and waits with trembling hands. He cannot control Himself. It is as if all His strength has left and He is filled with fear, feeling within, "What will happen if I do something wrong?"

Kṛṣṇa sees Śrīmatī Rādhārāṇī's form in the water of Rādhā-kuṇḍa. He sits on the bank of Rādhā-kuṇḍa and watches Her pastimes and interaction with the *sakhīs* and *mañjarīs* in the reflection of the water.

"How can I serve Her? How can I get permission?" Kṛṣṇa prays to the *sakhīs* and *mañjarīs* in a choked voice, with hairs standing on end and tears gently falling from His cheeks. The *sakhīs* come from another side and offer Kṛṣṇa peacock feathers and *guñjā-mālā*. Kṛṣṇa had fallen into an internal state of meditation. At the sound of the *gopīs*' words, His external sense returns and He feels, "I am very lucky today. Certainly they will give Me permission to serve and they will teach Me the proper process."

At this Rādhā-kuṇḍa, all special training, power, and taste is given to serve Rādhārāṇī.

14

Aśulka-Dāsikā

mādhavaṁ madana-keli-vibhrame
mattayā sarasijena bhavatyā
tāḍitaṁ sumukhi vīkṣya kintv iyaṁ
gūḍha-hāsya-vadanā bhaviṣyati
Vilāpa-kusumāñjali 78

O fair-faced one, when will I secretly smile, when I see You proudly and excitedly beating Mādhava with Your play lotus, in the flurry of Your amorous play?

Sometimes, while playing, Kṛṣṇa becomes perplexed and cannot understand who is who. Some of the *sakhīs* appear similar to Rādhārānī, and Kṛṣṇa becomes bewildered, "Who is Śrīmatī Rādhārānī and who is Rūpa, Rati, and the others?" Kṛṣṇa sometimes goes and addresses one of them, as if she is Rādhārānī, and then she becomes displeased. Then Kṛṣṇa understands, "Oh, I was mistaken. I have been defeated by the Vraja-devīs' beauty."

Mādhava is now defeated. He is not smiling. His face is dark and downcast. Seeing this, the *sakhīs* are also sad. They think, "How can we make Kṛṣṇa happy?"

They know that if Kṛṣṇa is not happy, Rādhārānī will never be happy, and the *sakhīs* want Śrīmatī Rādhārānī to always be happy.

su-lalita-nija-bāhv-āśliṣṭa-goṣṭhendra-sūnoḥ
su-valgutatara-bāhv-āśleṣa-divyan-natāṁsā
madhura-madana-gānaṁ tanvatī tena sārdhaṁ
subhaga-mukhi mudaṁ me hā kadā dāsyasi tvam
Vilāpa-kusumāñjali 79

> O beautiful-faced one, when will You give me great joy, singing sweet love songs with the prince of Vraja, while You embrace Him with Your graceful arms, and He places His strong arm on Your slender shoulder?

Kṛṣṇa plays with His friends at the foot of Govardhana. Suddenly He hears some singing from a distant forest garden. Where? In the area of Ratna-vedī, Ratna-siṁhāsana, and Gvāla-pokharā, nearby Kusuma-sarovara.

Kṛṣṇa becomes attracted. He thinks, "This singing is stealing My heart. The tone is fine and strong. It touches My heart and beckons Me there. It has a strong pull that I cannot resist."

"Stay here for a while," Kṛṣṇa tells the *sakhās*, "play and rest, or eat as you like. I'll come back in a few moments. I have some important business to attend."

Kṛṣṇa then walks towards the sound He heard. Many sounds are coming from inside, but how to go in? Kṛṣṇa tries again and again, but can't find the way in. The forest is deep, like a dark and thick jungle, but from within, Kṛṣṇa sees many sparkling lights and smells the sweet fragrance of many perfumes and flowers. The air is flowing gently, carrying the aroma and sound. Kṛṣṇa can tell a festival is going on inside and He tries to enter within, but cannot find any path inside.

"I wish I had wings," Kṛṣṇa thinks, "then I could fly in from above." He notices that peacocks and parrots are flying above the thick cluster of trees and are entering inside this *kuñja*. "What can I do?" Kṛṣṇa wonders. He then writes a message on a piece of paper. From where does He get paper? There are paper-trees in Vraja. Kṛṣṇa uses the bark of one of these trees, and with a fresh red mineral pigment from a stone near Govardhana, He writes His message and gives it to a peacock to carry into the *kuñja-kuṭīra*.

The peacock thinks, "If I deliver a message to these particular recipients from a sender of whom they do not approve, they will blacklist me from their grove. They will never allow me to come back and dance, play, and sing. They won't give me any further chance."

The peacock is in a dilemma. "I should not take this message," he considers, "but this person is also not ordinary. I have seen Him many times. He is special. Every day, He takes care of the cows and the forests of Vraja."

The poor peacock closes his eyes and contemplates what to do. He prays to the *gopīs*, but no answer comes.

"I will go outside for some time," he decides. "If I stay near this person without sending His message, He will be angry, and if I go inside to the Vraja-devīs, they will be angry. What should I do?"

The peacock, whose eyes are still closed, thinks to fly away from Kṛṣṇa, but he finds he has no strength to.

He gazes at Kṛṣṇa, as if asking, "Do you have some mystic power? Why can't I leave You?"

He begins to play and dance there with Kṛṣṇa, and meditates on the pastimes going on within the confidential *kuñja*.

"I was alone," Kṛṣṇa thinks, "but at least now there is a friendly peacock with Me. I will stay with him."

Then a little later, many other peacocks and birds come to Kṛṣṇa. Inside the *kuñja-kuṭīra* there is a wonderful festival going on, and now many deer, parrots, cuckoos, peacocks, squirrels, deer, and other animals start another program outside with Kṛṣṇa.

Suddenly the entrance to the *kuñja* opens and the Vraja-devīs come out and give *darśana* to Kṛṣṇa.

"This program of ours has no boundary and no guard," Kṛṣṇa tells them, "but why are you all so secretive? Our program is open. There is no fee. There is only one condition—if anyone comes here and watches this program, then when they next start a program, they must allow us to enter. Okay?"

The *mañjarīs* check with their mistress and the answer comes back as an emphatic, "No! Your program is useless. We are not interested in any males or animals. Our program is private. It is a special program for the *gopīs*, not for any *gopa*."

Kṛṣṇa tries to form some clever response, but they do not listen.

"This is not such an easy matter," they say. "Not everyone can enter Ratna-vedī, Ratna-siṁhāsana and Śyāma-talaiyā."

"What can one do to qualify for entrance and have *darśana* of the empress and to witness the festival here?" Kṛṣṇa inquires.

"Only *gopīs* are allowed here. And of the *gopīs*, no anti-parties are allowed! If anyone comes from Candrāvalī's party, they are not allowed entrance."

"Please give Me a chance," Kṛṣṇa says, "I am ready to pay any cost!"

"Alright," Lalitā and Viśākhā say, "we shall tell You how You can qualify for entrance. Anyone who comes inside this *kuñja* must continuously serve here and follow any order she is given. That person must have taken birth from the womb of a *gopī*, and have a *gopī* body. Entry here is permitted on these conditions."

The next day, Kṛṣṇa plays with His *sakhās* near that same area at the foot of Govardhana, and He again hears the wonderful singing coming from within the forest and follows it to that same secret *kuñja*.

Kṛṣṇa thinks, "Today I will get inside." He is more prepared today than yesterday. He saw the secret entrance when the *gopīs* came out to tease Him. But He didn't know how to unlock the gate. He discusses how to proceed with the peacocks and deer who are His close friends, and to His great delight, they somehow figure out how to open the gate.

"Kṛṣṇa," they say, "this gate only opens if you wear the dress of a *gopī* and you must know the names of Lalitā, Viśākhā, and the other senior *gopīs*. You must pray, evoking those names. This gate is very intelligent. You must have a deep desire to serve within and must pray for the mercy of the *gopīs*."

Kṛṣṇa now puts on the dress of a *gopī*. He takes many fragrant oils, *kājala*, combs, hairpins, ribbons, flower garlands, and many nice things, puts everything in a big basket and carries it on His head. He wears old tattered clothes, and His *svarūpa* is now that of a lady forest doctor.

He slowly approaches the entrance to the *kuñja*. He closes His eyes in deep prayer, says the names of the *aṣṭa-sakhīs*, and upon opening them, sees that the gate is open. He goes inside and becomes surprised.

"How amazing this *kuñja-kuṭīra* is!" He exclaims, "I have never seen anything so amazing!"

This place is in the heart of Girirāja Govardhana. It is said to be Girirāja's heart. On four sides, the slopes of Govardhana are seen, enclosing this secret *kuñja*.

Kṛṣṇa continues forward.

"Will they accept Me or not?" He worries and prays more.

Seeing some *gopīs*, He says in a soft, feminine voice, "If anyone is tired, I will massage them. I am a forest doctor. I know the art of using herbs to remove all exhaustion and to uplift one. I also know how to comb and decorate the hair nicely. I took training for a long time. Now I hear that the Vraja-devīs are in need of a servant like Me. Therefore, I have come as an *aśulka-dāsikā*, unpaid maidservant. I need no pay. But I have only one request, if My service is pleasing, then please accept My help not only once, but daily."

Rati Mañjarī takes this message to Rūpa Mañjarī, and Rūpa Mañjarī tells Lalitā-devī, who says, "Very well. Let her first serve a *mañjarī*, and if that *mañjarī* approves of the quality of her service, then she can gradually gain entrance into serving the *sakhīs*, and finally we may allow her to serve our Śvāmini."

The *mañjarīs* became afraid, "No! We don't need any service. This *dāsī* should go and serve Rādhārānī directly."

Rādhārānī is sitting on a raised seat, in the heart of the beautiful program being held in Her enchanting *kuñja*. She has been dancing and singing for some time and Her hair is slightly disheveled and Her ornaments misplaced.

With permission, this new *dāsī* goes forward and begins to delicately massage Śrīmatī Rādhārānī with a herbal ointment. Rādhārānī immediately feels pleased. Then the *dāsī* gives a drop of some other medicine in the nose of Śrīmatī Rādhārānī, who finds the smell of the herbs very soothing. This new *dāsī* then arranges a bed, combs Her hair, and massages Her feet. Rādhārānī becomes very happy.

"This girl is My dear friend," She says, "she has served Me so nicely. Her bodily shine, nature, and behavior is good—everything about Her is good, but Her dress is very dirty and tattered."

Śrīmatī Rādhārānī orders the *mañjarīs*, "I have many new dresses. Go fetch something and I will give our new friend a nice outfit. Bring something quickly and we will dress her."

"No, no, no," the new *dāsī* says, "this is not a good idea. I haven't started any business here. I am serving without any selfish motive. The old dress is good for Me. If I wear a new fancy dress, no one will give Me any service. I am a poor humble beggar. This is good for Me. If I become popular, famous, rich, healthy, and wealthy, then no one will give Me any service. I like this dress that I have."

"No!" Rādhārānī says, "catch her and give her a bath in the sweet waters of Śyāma-talaiyā. After this, bathe Her once more in Kusuma-sarovara, and then bring Her back here to be given fresh clothes and new jewelry."

"How can I accept? I have never taken reciprocation for service in My life."

"How then do You sustain Your life?" Rādhārānī asks.

"The Vrajavāsīs' love and affection is My food and more than sufficient for My maintenance. I take nothing else in exchange for My service. I go from house to house serving the Vrajavāsīs, and they mercifully give Me some buttermilk. I take this to sustain Myself."

Hearing this, the Vraja-devīs smile. "Truly we have met a very honest and principled girl—such a nice *aśulka-dāsikā*. This is a *dāsī* of the highest class. From today You will be Rādhārānī's permanent servant. You should come daily to serve Her."

Kṛṣṇa in His disguise becomes overjoyed and dances in ecstasy.

"But," Rādhārānī says, "if you want to come every day, you must be like the other *sakhīs* and *mañjarīs*. You can't wear this foul dress around us! You must bathe and wear a nice cloth. And we will give you Kṛṣṇa's *prasāda* to maintain your life. Only drinking buttermilk will not do."

Śrīmatī Rādhārānī turns to Her *sakhīs* and says, "Eating Kṛṣṇa's *praśāda* will make this Dāsī healthy and a proper member of our company, wouldn't you agree?" The *sakhīs* and *mañjarī* agree enthusiastically, and then suddenly grab the new *dāsī* and forcibly take her to Śyāma-talaiya for a bath. Just as they begin removing her garments, Kṛṣṇa wriggles free, jumps in the lake, and swims away as fast as He can. He emerges, surfaces on the other side, and then runs off into the forest.

jitvā pāśāka-khelāyām
ācchidya muralīṁ hareḥ
kṣiptāṁ mayi tvayā devi
gopayiṣyāmi tāṁ kadā

Vilāpa-kusumāñjali 80

O Devī, when will You defeat Hari in a dice game, snatch away His flute and toss it to me so that I can hide it somewhere?

The *sakhīs* are amused, "What a strange girl! She had wide shoulders and a strong body, but Her hands were soft and She spoke sweetly."

This new girl remained in the thoughts of the *sakhīs* and *mañjarīs*. "It would be nice if that *dāsī* comes again," they say.

"Which village did she come from?" they ask each other. "Where does she live? Why didn't you ask her?"

A little later, the *sakhīs* come out of their secret grove and see a large group of *sakhās* playing with Kṛṣṇa near Gvāla-pokharā. The *gopīs* look, and see that Kṛṣṇa's *muralī* is tucked in His waist belt. One *mañjarī* dashes forward and snatches Kṛṣṇa's *muralī*, runs off, and gives it to Śrīmatī. Śrīmatī first hides the *muralī* in Her long hair, and then decides to hide it in Her bodice so that Kṛṣṇa cannot take it.

Kṛṣṇa becomes distressed at the loss of His *muralī*. The *mañjarīs* go forward and ask Him, "O Kṛṣṇa, as You were playing here with Your friends, might You have seen a new girl run by? She came to serve Śrīmatī in our grove and then abruptly left. Did You see Her and perhaps know where She came from? She was an excellent *dāsī*. We want her to know that Rādhārāṇī was very pleased with her service. If You can tell us where she is then we will return Your *muralī*."

"I know of Her," Kṛṣṇa replies. "She has one request. She desires to serve Rādhārāṇī daily, but without any pay. If you agree not to give her any new cloth or ornaments, then she will come and serve. The only payment she wants is to have the feet of Rādhārānī placed on her head."

After a pause, Kṛṣṇa asks, "Now will you please give back My *muralī?*" "You must first call that *dāsī* here. Śrīmatī is anxious to know where she is. Please invite her to come."

Kṛṣṇa wonders what to do. "Okay," He says, "let us arrange a match. The losing party will follow the wishes of the winning party."

The Vraja-devīs accept Kṛṣṇa's challenge and prepare for the game. In the meantime, Kṛṣṇa disappears behind a tree and dons a worn out old dress He had found and comes forth as the *aśulka-dāsikā*.

When they see Her, the Vraja-devīs exclaim, "Oh, it is Her!"

They confer amongst themselves, "We will catch and bind her, so she can never leave our company."

The *gopīs* catch Kṛṣṇa and then bring Him and bind His cloth to Rādhikā's. They are then called Rādhā-Dāmodara. At this time, the Vraja-devīs give Kṛṣṇa permission to serve Śrīmatī in all manners. Then, when He tries to leave, they say, "It is not possible. If anyone comes once to serve Śrīmatī, my Rādhārānī gives permanent shelter. She cannot leave then. How will You return to Your past life and ways?"

Kṛṣṇa tries to leave, but the *gopīs* refuse to let Him go.

> *ayi sumukhi kadāhaṁ mālatī-keli-talpe*
> *madhura-madhura-goṣṭhīṁ bibhratīṁ vallabhena*
> *manasija-sukhade 'smin mandire smera-gaṇḍaṁ*
> *sa-pulaka-tanu-veśā tvām kadā vījayāmi*
>
> *Vilāpa-kusumāñjali* 81

O fair-faced one, when, with my body rippling in ecstasy, will I fan You, as You lie on a playbed of *mālatī* flowers in the temple of the bliss of amorous love, smiling and conversing sweetly with Your beloved?

Dāsa Gosvāmī prays, "O fair-faced one, the splendid temple of Cupid is decorated with flowers. The new *sevikā* is there with a *cāmara*, fanning Śrīmatī and sometimes massaging Her feet. How will I learn there, and wait there to please Rādhārāṇī?"

Rādhārāṇī says again and again to Her *sakhīs* and *mañjarīs*, "Give this new *dāsī* some gift. She is doing everything for My happiness. She will soon be expert and I will offer her in the service of Kṛṣṇa. I will invite Kṛṣṇa here and this new *sakhī* will go to serve Him. She knows how to decorate with flowers and make them into garlands. She knows how to dress and massage and how to speak humbly and sweetly."

Kṛṣṇa offers Himself in Rādhārāṇī's service. He teaches this service of Śrīmatī Rādhārāṇī. If He doesn't teach this service, how can anyone learn to serve Śrīmatījī?

Rādhārāṇī will not say, "Follow Me. Serve Me like this." But Kṛṣṇa Himself adopts the form of a *mañjarī* and teaches this service. Śrīmatī doesn't order the *sakhīs* and *mañjarīs* to serve Her. They naturally serve and everything they do is perfect. But if Kṛṣṇa performs this service to Rādhikā and teaches it Himself, then it is more sweet and attractive.

After serving, Kṛṣṇa fans Rādhārāṇī and then disappears. When He goes, Śrīmatī feels great separation. This separation cannot be tolerated or fathomed.

Therefore, Bhaktivinoda Ṭhākura says, "I cannot tolerate Śrīmatī Rādhārāṇī feeling separation from Kṛṣṇa for one moment."

śrī kṛṣṇa-virahe, rādhikāra daśā, āmi to' sahite nāri
yugala-milana, sukhera kāraṇa, jīvana chāḍite pāri

Śrī Gītāmālā, siddhi-lālasa, song 10

I am absolutely unable to tolerate Śrī Rādhikā's pitiable condition when She is suffering in separation from Śrī Kṛṣṇa, but I am fully prepared to immediately give up my life for the sake of Their happy reunion.

The Vraja-devīs say, "When Kṛṣṇa comes, also serve Him."

"No," the new *dāsī* says, "I have taken a vow only to serve Śrīmatī Rādhārānī. Without Her service, I will not serve any other. I never look at the face of any man. I will not look, talk or meet with any man. This is not My business and nature. I will not share My love with any other. I only like Śrīmatī Rādhārānī. I am only waiting for Her footdust and a drop of Her love. I don't like anything else."

āyātodyat-kamala-vadane hanta līlābhisārād
gaty-āṭopaiḥ śrama-vilulitaṁ devi pādābja-yugmam
snehāt samvāhayitum api hrī-puñja-mūrte 'py alajjaṁ
nāma-grāhaṁ nija-janam imaṁ hā kadā notsyasi tvam

Vilāpa-kusumāñjali 82

O Devī, O You whose face is a blossoming lotus flower, O personification of shyness, when, Your two lotus feet exhausted from walking to the rendezvous place, will You affectionately call me by name and engage me in massaging Your feet?

"O lotus faced one, sometimes, before *līlā-abhisāra*, You come walking gracefully, and Your feet become a little tired. When will You mercifully call me, 'Rati, please come. I have come from a long distance. Massage my feet.' I am very dear to Her, therefore She speaks like this with me. I will think, 'Today I am very fortunate. Śrīmatī has given me permission to serve.' Rādhārānī is very shy. She never tells anyone to serve Her. She only remembers *kṛṣṇa-nāma* and serves Kṛṣṇa. But today, She affectionately tells me, 'Rati Mañjarī, please massage My feet.'

"I will apply ointment on Śrīmatī's soft lotus feet. Śrīmatī will ask me, 'O Rati, where did you learn this? At the time of *abhisāra*, you must come with Me and wait upon Me.' O Devī, I will wash Your lotus feet with nectar from lotus flowers.

I will perform *abhiṣeka* of Your feet with milk, yogurt, ghee, and other pure substances. This will be very soothing to Your tired feet."

hā naptri rādhe tava sūrya-bhakteḥ
kālaḥ samutpanna itaḥ kuto 'si
itīva roṣān mukharā lapantī
sudheva kiṁ māṁ sukhayiṣyatīha

Vilāpa-kusumāñjali 83

"O grand-daughter Rādhe, the time for You to worship the sun has come! Where are You?" When will I hear these cross words of Mukharā-devī which are like nectar to my ears?

Mukharā, the grandmother of Śrīmatī Rādhikā, says, "O Rādhe, don't You know it is time to worship the sun? Where have You been? Why are You sitting here aimlessly? What are You thinking of? Go quickly. The time is passing. Worship the sun. It is almost mid-day. Hurry!"

Kṛṣṇa is coming on the side of Govardhana; He is midway. Śrīmatī Rādhārānī goes there to arrange everything, and *rasika-śekhara* Kṛṣṇa is coming to meet with Her.

devi bhāṣita-pīyūṣaṁ smitakarpūra vāsitam
śrotrābhyāṁ nayanābhyāṁ te kiṁ nu seviṣyate mayā

Vilāpa-kusumāñjali 84

O Devī, when will I serve Your nectarful words with my ears and Your camphor-scented smile with my eyes?

Dāsa Gosvāmī says, "O Devī, hearing this sweet nectarful instruction from Mukharā, You become surprised and say, 'Oh, I did not realize it was so late. I have not arranged anything yet.' "

Śrīmatī Rādhārānī then notices that the *sakhīs* and *mañjarīs* have already prepared everything for the *pūjā*. She has come back from Nandagrāma and is waiting in Varsānā, remembering the morning's pastimes. Her father, mother and everyone know that it is time for Her to go and worship the sun at Sūrya-kuṇḍa.

Vṛṣabhānu Mahārāja wishes to arrange a horse or bullock cart. Her uncles agree and say to Her, "We will arrange a cart for you to ride on."

"No," She declines.

"A palanquin then."

"No."

"Oh, it is only a few minutes from here," Mukharā says, "why don't You just walk? Walking will make You strong. Being carried around everywhere is not good."

The hidden meaning of her words are, "If Rādhārānī is in a palanquin, She will be hidden and all those unable to have Her *darśana* will be upset. If She goes by foot, then the Vrajavāsīs' hearts will be very happy. They are all waiting for Rādhārānī's *darśana*. This *darśana* is very helpful for everyone."

> ***kusuma-cayana-khelāṁ kurvatī tvaṁ parītā***
> ***rasa-kuṭila-sakhībhiḥ prāṇa-nāthena sārdham***
> ***kapaṭa-kalaha-kelyā kvāpi roṣeṇa bhinnā***
> ***mama mudam ati-velāṁ dhāsyase su-vrate kim***
>
> *Vilāpa-kusumāñjali* 85

> O pious one, when, picking flowers with Your sweet and crooked friends, You angrily quarrel with the Lord of Your life, will You fill me with boundless happiness?

Dāsa Gosvāmī says, "O Rādhikā, Your vow is firm. As You walk, many *gopīs* come from different villages and follow Your footsteps. How can You meet with Kṛṣṇa? For this purpose,

You go in the garden to pick flowers and quarrel with Kṛṣṇa there and become angry at Him."

"Hey! Don't pick these flowers," Kṛṣṇa's party says.

"Why not?" the *gopīs* say.

"This is My garden."

"No! This is not Your garden."

"My father is the king of Vraja. That makes Me the prince and this garden is therefore mine."

"No! This garden is Vṛndā-Devī's. We will pick flowers here whether You like it or not."

"I won't let You disturb a single flower."

"You and Your friends are like elephant cubs, coming every day to smash and destroy Vraja's gardens. You are not worried about the flowers' well-being. We take care of all this. But when we pick a few flowers, You come to quarrel with us."

Kṛṣṇa and the Vraja-devīs have these kinds of quarrels over flowers. "You are thieves!" Kṛṣṇa says, "you are stealing My flowers. You are breaking the creepers and branches of the trees and destroying the garden. I will have to arrest you all and put you in My jail."

"How big is this jail of Yours?"

"I have big chains and I shall bind you with them," Kṛṣṇa says. Another meaning of these words is, "I will take you in My arms, embrace you, and place you in My heart forever. No one will be able to rescue you from My heart."

Kṛṣṇa continues, "This person who is now fighting is certainly Candrāvalī, the goddess of anger. This is not my worshipable Rādhā! She has no anger like this. If anyone has this fire, she is definitely Candrāvalī!"

Kṛṣṇa teases Rādhārānī like this, and the *sakhās* all begin to laugh and clap. Then the *gopīs* become angry and run away from the flower garden.

15

Quite Contrary

nānā-vidhaiḥ pṛthula-kāku-bharair asāhyaiḥ
samprārthitaḥ priyatayā bata mādhavena
tvan-māna-bhaṅga-vidhaye sa-daye jano 'yaṁ
vyāgraḥ patiṣyati kadā lalitā-padānte

Vilāpa-kusumāñjali 86

O merciful one, when, sweetly begged by Mādhava with many unbearable appeals, will this agitated person fall down before Lalitā's feet to plead on His behalf and break Your jealous anger?

Kṛṣṇa begs Śrīmatī Rādhārāṇī again and again to forgive Him, saying, "O kind-hearted Rādhike, I have come here for Your *darśana* and to hear some sweet words from You. But You are angry with Me. O merciful Rādhe, please forgive Me. I am the small servant of Your servants. When will You be pleased with Me?"

But Śrīmatī Rādhārāṇī remains determined not to show Him favor. Then He goes to Lalitā-devī. He offers *praṇāma* and requests her, "O Lalitā-devī, you are very merciful and great. Please pray to Śrīmatī Rādhārāṇī for My sake. May She be pleased with Me and accept Me as Her own. Please do something."

Lalitā-devī only chastises Kṛṣṇa. Then, with a mood of deep repentance, Mādhava goes to Rati Mañjarī and says in great sadness, "O Rati, I now take shelter of you. I promise that I never made any offense. I never insulted Your Svāminī. Why is She angry with Me? Alas! What can I do now? She is generally so affectionate, loving and kind, but why is She so hard on Me today? She is trying to break the soft heart of another. This is great cruelty. I can't tolerate this any longer.

"Alas! Alas! Yamarāja is coming swiftly to take Me away, for I can no longer live in this separation from Śrīmatī Rādhārāṇī."

Hearing this, Rati Mañjarī cannot tolerate Kṛṣṇa's distress. Śrīmatī Rādhārāṇī has been listening to everything, and She now speaks to Her *sakhīs* and *mañjarīs*, "Who is this person? Why is He crying and weeping here? Where has He come from? Before, this *kuñja-kuṭīra* was clean and peaceful, but now this person's lamenting has made this place impure and full of distress. Only singing and dancing can lift this dark weight from our *kuñja*. Otherwise this place will become even darker and a cosmic devastation will occur. Therefore, start a nice program."

Then the Vraja-devīs begin to sing and dance.

prītyā maṅgala-gīta-nṛtya-vilasad-
vīṇādi-vādyotsavaiḥ
śuddhānāṁ payasāṁ ghaṭair bahu-vidhaiḥ
saṁvāsitānāṁ bhṛśam
vṛndāraṇya-mahādhipatya-vidhaye yaḥ
paurṇamāsyā svayaṁ
dhīre saṁvihitaḥ sa kiṁ tava mahotseko
mayā drakṣyate

Vilāpa-kusumāñjali 87

O calm, grave one, when will I witness Your great ceremonial bathing, as You are being crowned as the queen of Vṛndāvana by Paurṇamāsī? Your coronation will be celebrated with a great festival of love, with auspicious singing, dancing, and the playing of *vīṇās* and other instruments, while You are being bathed with many pitchers of pure, scented water?

Paurṇamāsī-devī begins a festival of auspicious songs for the pleasure of Vraja's empress. The *gopīs* begin to dance and sing, while playing many musical instruments like the sitar.

They then arrange drinks in big clay pots and begin Śrīmatī Rādhārānī's *mahā-abhiṣeka*. At the time of Her *abhiṣeka*, they sing, while playing on many instruments on the order of Paurṇamāsī-devī.

Kṛṣṇa then bathes Himself with the *caraṇāmṛta* of Śrīmatī Rādhārānī and all His blackness and impurity is washed away. All hardness, blackness, and sadness is cleansed and washed out of the *kuñja* and Vraja-maṇḍala.

Mahāprabhu says, '*Ceto darpanan marjanama*—how can you clean your heart? This is only possible by:

bhakta-pada-dhūli āra bhakta-pada-jala
bhakta-bhukta-avaśeṣa – ei tina mahābala
Caitanya-caritāmṛta, Antya-līlā 16.60

The foot-dust of a devotee, the water that has washed his feet and the remnants of food left by him are three very powerful items that help one progress in *sādhana-bhakti*.

The only way the heart can be cleansed is by taking the *caraṇāmṛta* of Śrīmatī Rādhārānī or Her beloved followers. The dust from their feet is *vraja-raja*; this is what makes Vraja so special. Vraja is known as *va-raja*. *Va* means 'special' and *raja* means 'dust'.

Kṛṣṇa always rolls in this dust and smears it on His body. He takes the Vraja-devīs' *caraṇāmṛta*, remnants, and foot dust, and distributes it. By this process, the heart is easily purified and illuminated.

Helpful, loveful, hopeful, merciful, blessful, and very powerful Śrīmatī Rādhārānī has tolerance and patience, and She knows everything. She does not reject anyone. When Kṛṣṇa is nearby Her, He is very happy, and when He is a little disconnected with Her, then He becomes dry, Brahma.

Śakti-śaktimator-abheda, Rādhā-Kṛṣṇa are inseparable. Therefore Kṛṣṇa never wants to go an inch away from

svarūpa-śakti, Śrīmatī Rādhārāṇī. She is sweet and humble and maintains all living entities with Her potency.

Paurṇamāsī-devī gives everyone in the *kuñja-kuṭīra* a chance to serve Rādhārāṇī during Her *mahā-abhiṣeka*. Some serve by singing, some by dancing, some by playing instruments, and some by bathing Her directly. They use camphor, *aguru*, *kastūrī*, and arrange many full pots of water with these fragrances inside to start Rādhārāṇī's *mahā-abhiṣeka*.

After this *abhiṣeka*, everything in Vraja-maṇḍala becomes joyful and surcharged by the potency of Her *caraṇāmṛta*. Drinking this nectar, Pṛthvī-devī blossoms in joy.

Dāsa Gosvāmī prays to be there, assisting in the *mahā-abhiṣeka* of Śrīmatī Rādhārāṇī, and receiving Her *caraṇāmṛta*.

bhrātrā go-'yutam atra mañju-vadane snehena dattvālayaṁ
śrīdāmnā kṛpaṇāṁ pratoṣya jaṭilāṁ rakṣākhya-rākā-kṣaṇe
nītāyāh sukha-śoka-rodana-bharais te sāndravantyāḥ paraṁ
vātsalyāj janakau vidhāsyata itaḥ kiṁ lālanaṁ me 'grataḥ

Vilāpa-kusumāñjali 88

> O fair-faced one, will I be present on Rakṣā Pūrṇimā, the full-moon day in the month of Śravaṇa, when Your brother Śrīdāmā comes to Yāvaṭa, with ten thousand cows to satisfy the greedy Jaṭilā, and he affectionately takes You along to Varsānā, where Your parents lovingly fondle You in front of me, as You melt with weeping from both happiness and sorrow?

Jaṭilā is very greedy for wealth. She is a great miser. On Baladeva's birthday, Rākhi Pūrṇimā, she tries to stop Rādhārāṇī from going to Her father's house in Varsānā. Why? She knows that if Rādhārāṇī stays at her house, then Vṛṣabhānu Mahārāja will send many gifts for his beloved daughter. Not only Her father, but Lalitā, Viśākhā, and everyone in Vraja-maṇḍala will send Her many presentations, like sweets, cloth, and ornaments.

Greedy Jaṭilā thinks, "If Rādhārāṇī goes to Her father's house, nothing will come for me. When Rādhārāṇī is present, my cows give a lot of milk, and so much wealth automatically comes. But when She leaves, everything becomes dry."

Śrīdāma approaches Jaṭilā and says, "Listen, I will give you thousands of cows in charity. Please allow my sister to come to Varsānā. I have come to ask this of you."

Hearing this news, Śrīmatī Rādhārāṇī becomes overjoyed. She is anxious, "When will I go and meet with My parents? When will I meet with grandmother?" Her heart is very soft and She begins to weep in separation from Her parents.

Rati Mañjarī says, "I will go there and request the greedy mother-in-law of my Svāminī, 'O Jaṭilā, how many cows do you want? I will tell Vṛṣabhānu Mahārāja and his brothers, and they will give you as many cows as you want. Just please give permission for Rādhārāṇī to go to Her father's house. Today is Rakṣā-bandhana. Rādhārāṇī will go and bind a bracelet on Her brother's wrist, and he will give Her cloth, ornaments, and many new gifts. Please give permission."

But Jaṭilā at first does not agree. "I will ask my son," she says, "if he agrees, then I will consider granting permission. I will also ask my daughter. If they agree, then I will give permission."

Abhimanyu has great reverence for Śrīmatī Rādhikā and always keeps a respectful distance from Her. When Brahmā stole the calves and boys and put them in a cave, Kṛṣṇa Himself took on their forms for a year. He became Abhimanyu and all the *sakhās*, and in their forms, married all the *gopīs*. When the real Abhimanyu returned after a year, he asked his mother,

"How has Rādhārāṇī come to our house? Why is She here?"

"What do you mean?" Jaṭilā said, "She is your wife."

"No, how is that possible! She is highly respectable," Abhimanyu said. "She is the daughter of Vṛṣabhānu Mahārāja, the king of Varsānā. I am very lowly."

Abhimanyu was in the cave for one year and did not know he was meant to have married to Rādhārānī. He came back and offered *praṇāma* to Śrīmatī Rādhārānī, and hearing they were married, he said, "No, this can't be true."

The next day he again asked, "How did Rādhārānī come to my house? Why is She here?"

He heard, "When you were in the mouth of Aghāsura, you became affected by the monster's poison and fell lifeless. Then Kṛṣṇa requested Rādhārānī to go help you and remove all the poisonous effect. She then came and gave you new life."

Hearing this, Abhimanyu respected Her even more, saying, "Oh, She gave me new life? She is a worshipable goddess."

From that time, Abhimanyu stayed outside in a small hut and did not reside in the house. Every day, after milking the cows, he brings many gifts and puts them at the door of Rādhārānī's room. He offers *praṇāma* there, and returns to his hut.

"Won't you stay in the house?" Jaṭilā and Kuṭilā ask him.

"No, this house is not mine. It is Rādhārānī's house. She is Vṛṣabhānu-rāja-nandinī and is very respectable. She is worshiped by everyone in Vraja-maṇḍala."

Abhimanyu stays outside as a guard and gatekeeper. Even Brahmā comes to worship Śrīmatī Rādhārānī. Abhimanyu has knowledge of Her glories; therefore Rādhārānī was safe there. In Varsānā, there could be some difficulty meeting Kṛṣṇa, with Her parents and family all there. But in Yāvaṭa, Rādhārānī is alone with Her *sakhīs* and *mañjarīs*. She is safe and protected, as others have no *adhikāra* to enter there.

Sometimes Kṛṣṇa comes to Yāvaṭa in the dress of Abhimanyu. Jaṭilā and Kuṭilā are then overjoyed to see Him entering Śrīmatī's room.

"This is very good," says Jaṭilā. "I am happy that finally Abhimanyu is spending time with Rādhārānī."

On Rākhi Pūrṇimā, Śrīdāma asked permission for Rādhārānī to come with him to the house of Her father. For a long time She has not met with Vṛṣabhānu and Her mother Kīrtidā-devī.

When Jaṭilā's greed is satisfied, she allows Rādhārānī to return home for sometime. Rādhārānī goes home with Śrīdāma. There, Kīrtidā-devī takes Rādhārānī in her arms and smells Her head. Then Her father asks Her, "Do You like Yāvaṭa or Varsānā? If You like Varsānā, I will never leave You. You will stay here. O my dear daughter, You are the pupil of our eyes. Without You, we have no light."

She is very happy to see Her family after so long, but She is also upset. "You didn't send Me any news," She says, "and you didn't come to see Me."

Because of this, She cries while meeting with Her father and mother.

lajjayāli-purataḥ parato māṁ
gāhvaraṁ giri-pater bata nītvā
divya-gānam api tat-svara-bhedaṁ
śikṣayiṣyasi kadā sa-daye tvam

Vilāpa-kusumāñjali 89

O merciful one, when, because I feel shy before Your friends, will You take me to a cave at Govardhana and tutor me in the art of singing?

Dāsa Gosvāmī says, "O Rādhike, please take me inside the caves of Girirāja Govardhana and teach me how to sing, teach me how to play the *vīṇā*, and guitar. I cannot learn from anyone else. Please take me alone inside a cave of Girirāja Govardhana and there teach me how to sing and play beautiful melodies."

Songs are of many kinds. One kind is for the happiness of others, and another kind is for lifting the spirits of a person who is sad. Another type of singing is such that its hearer will become very hungry and eager to eat. Another type of song will make you want to play sports. Sports players like to hear this kind of music as they play. And in the military, while preparing to fight, soldiers like to hear music that is dangerous and ferocious, like lions roaring.

Sometimes, when there is no rain although the long expected clouds travel overhead, the appropriate song must be sung, and then it begins to rain. Such prayers are found in the Sāma-Veda.

When Kṛṣṇa sleeps, there is one type of song to sing. When He wakes, there is another type of song, and while He eats there is another. When He sets out with the cows, His *sakhās* make happy music behind Him. The cows and calves bound around blissfully, the birds fly very fast, and all creatures are thus involved in a grand musical festival in the forest. Even the trees begin to dance, hearing the joyous musical celebration as Kṛṣṇa passes them. It seems as if the trees will jump out of the ground and run along with Him.

yācitā lalitayā kila devyā
lajjayā nata-mukhīṁ gaṇato mām
devi divya-rasa-kāvya-kadambaṁ
pāṭhayiṣyasi kadā praṇayena

Vilāpa-kusumāñjali 90

O Devī, when, requested by Lalitā-devī, will You affectionately ask me, my head bowed with shyness in the assembly, to recite many splendid and sweet poems?

Dāsa Gosvāmī prays, "O Rādhike, when will You accept me into the group of Your near and dear *sakhīs,* and ask me to sing poetry for Your pleasure? How can I learn this art of sweet service? Please teach me. I will go to Your class. I will learn from You which poem to sing at which time, with which melody."

nija-kuṇḍa-taṭi-kuñje guñjad-bhramara-saṅkule
devi tvaṁ kacchapī-śikṣāṁ kadā māṁ kārayiṣyasi
Vilāpa-kusumāñjali 91

O Devī, when will You teach me to play the *kacchapī*, in a grove, filled with humming bees, on the shore of Your lake?"

At Rādhā-kuṇḍa, there are many honeybees that drink so much nectar from the lotus flowers that they are unable to return to their hive. They sleep in the lotus flowers, having become intoxicated by drinking their nectar. This signifies that, if anyone comes to Rādhā-kuṇḍa and just once gets a chance to serve Rādhārāṇī, then they cannot go back. Even Parabrahma came and doesn't want to ever leave.

Many *kuñja-kuṭīras* are present at this Rādhā-kuṇḍa. "When will You call me inside one of these *kuñja-kuṭīras* and instruct me to play the *kacchapī*? At such a time, Kṛṣṇa will come from a distance to hear the music.

vihārais truṭitaṁ hāraṁ gumphitaṁ dayitaṁ kadā
sakhīnāṁ lajjayā devi saṁjñayā māṁ nidekṣyasi
Vilāpa-kusumāñjali 92

O Devī, when will You, being shy before Your *sakhīs*, hint that I should re-string Your favorite necklace, which was broken in Your pastimes?

Raghunātha dāsa Gosvāmī now prays, "O Devī Rādhike, You are now playing *kandarpa-līlā* with Kṛṣṇa. Your necklace breaks in the course of this game, and this I will fix. You are very shy and will not tell anyone. But You give me a hint, and I step forward to carefully fix Your necklace."

At Rādhā-kuṇḍa, one *kuñja-kuṭīra* is for wrestling matches between the Divine Couple. In one of their matches, Śrīmatī's necklace breaks. Pearls and jewels scatter here and there.

It is difficult to fix the necklace. If one pearl is misplaced, the color pattern changes and the beautiful harmony is lost. On Your indication, I will go and fix Your necklace very carefully.

sva-mukhān man-mukhe devi
kadā tāmbūla-carvitam
snehāt sarva-diśo vīkṣya
samaye tvaṁ pradāsyasi

Vilāpa-kusumāñjali 93

O Devī, when, after looking in all directions, will You take the chewed betelnuts from Your mouth and affectionately place them in my mouth?

Dāsa Gosvāmī now prays, "O Rādhike, You are very kind. Please mercifully give me the remnants of *tāmbūla* that You have chewed."

There are many *mañjarīs*, like Lavaṅga Mañjarī, Guṇa Mañjarī, Bhānu Mañjarī, Rati Mañjarī, Rūpa Mañjarī, and so forth. Rati Mañjarī stays with that group. Anything she gets, she distributes and then takes the last part herself. She does not take anything independently.

A proper *guru-sevaka* does not independently accept or digest the things that come to him. Sharing is part of the process of Vaiṣṇavism. If one receives anything, it should be shared appropriately.

16

I am Yours

Kṛṣṇa is Parabrahma, Paramātmā, Parameśvara—the Supreme Lord. If God Himself suffers and cannot be peaceful for a second without the grace of Śrīmatī Rādhārānī when She is angry with Him, then what will be the position of the living entities if they are divided and distant from Her? Thus, if any conditioned soul chants the holy names of Śrīmatī Rādhārānī, remembers Her, prays for Her blessings, and cries for Her compassion, then certainly, without a doubt, such a person will experience eternal bliss. He himself will be blissful, and will fill anyone who comes in contact with him in bliss.

kenāpi doṣa-lava-mātra-lavena devi
santāḍyamāna iha dhīra-mate tvayoccaiḥ
roṣeṇa tal lalitayā kila nīyamānaḥ
sandrakṣyate kim u manāk sa-dayaṁ jano 'yam

Vilāpa-kusumāñjali 95

O grave and sober one, You once severely rebuked me and sent me away for committing just the tiniest mistake. When will you mercifully glance upon this pitiful person after Lalitā brings her back to You?

Dāsa Gosvāmī prays, "O Rādhike, please do not be angry with me. You are the epitome of patience and tolerance. In this world, millions of people don't follow or respect You. Still, You continuously help all living entities, but they do not think of You. You don't reject them or stop nourishing them for even a second. If You did so, all the material and spiritual creation would be destroyed in an instant. You have unlimited patience and give everything to the living entities. I am full of faults. Please don't look at them.

"Please send Lalitā-devī. May she be kind to me and bring me before You, and then ask You to forgive me and bestow some service on this small Rati. I do not understand what is wrong and what is right. If You say, 'Get out, never come near Me. You have no brain,' then what will be my position? I don't know the process of Your service, but I am very greedy for this."

Absorbed in his eternal form as Rati Mañjarī, Dāsa Gosvāmī prays to Śrīmatī Rādhārāṇī, "O Rādhike, I made a small mistake and therefore You have kicked me out of Your *kuñja*. Kṛṣṇa came and spoke to me, questioning me and enticing me to reply. I tried very hard to remain silent, but afterwards I could not constrain myself and I independently gave an answer to Him. Seeing me speaking with Kṛṣṇa outside the *kuñja*, You became angry. When I reentered the *kuñja*, You said, 'Get out! Don't come near me.' Lalitā-devī saw me crying in a corner and brought me back to You. O Rādhe, my heart was broken when You sent me away angrily. I cannot express the magnitude of my sorrow and cannot find peace anywhere. I have no one in this world but You; I cannot leave You and go to anyone else. O Rādhe, I had no desire to speak with Kṛṣṇa, but what could I do..."

Śrīla Gurudeva gave an example here. Once, Vallabhācārya instructed his dear disciple, "When Ṭhākurajī is given rest after the midday offering and *ārati*, go inside the temple altar and fan the Lord with eyes closed. If you hear someone saying anything, don't give any answer or open your eyes."

The disciple followed his Gurudeva's instruction. A short while after beginning to fan the Lord, the disciple heard someone saying, "Hey! Why are you fanning for so long with closed eyes? Open your eyes and look at Me!"

When the disciple didn't open his eyes or speak anything, the voice continued, "Speak something! You will fan Me, but won't talk to Me, or look at Me? If you have so much daring to fan Me as I rest, then why won't you speak to Me?"

But the disciple remained firm to the order of his Gurudeva and remained fanning, while the Lord endeavored to make him speak. Outside, Gurudeva was waiting to see what happened.

When the Deitie's curtains were opened at four in the afternoon, Vallabhācārya asked his disciple, "Who was talking to you?"

"Gurudeva, I followed your instruction and didn't open my eyes. But someone was saying again and again, 'Open your eyes and talk to Me.'"

"You did well."

Śrīla Gurudeva gave this example when commenting on this verse of *Vilāpa-kusumāñjali.*

Śrīla Gurudeva would further explain.

Kṛṣṇa could not tolerate seeing Rādhārānī's one-pointed beloved maidservant. She was so close to Rādhārānī, such an expert maidservant, and so beautiful, that Kṛṣṇa came and tried to converse with Rati Mañjarī, teasing her from behind, in front, and side-to-side. Rati Mañjarī remained firm and ignored Kṛṣṇa, and then He began teasing her, "O Svāminī's beloved! O Svāminī's nearest and dearest! There is no one dearer to Her than you. You know Her better than any other. You are so chaste! You don't speak with anyone else or look at anyone. Oh! You are so proud. If anyone comes to you, you show them contempt and reject them."

Kṛṣṇa began teasing her like this more and more, until finally Rati Mañjarī's resolve was broken and she strongly responded to Kṛṣṇa's antics. This is called *vaco-vegam.*

Rādhārānī had told Rati Mañjarī, "You are so close to Me, don't allow any distance to come between us. Don't speak or make relation with anyone."

Rādhārānī knew what had transpired. When Rati Mañjarī fearfully came to Rādhārānī, She reprimanded her, "Why did you give Him a moment of your time? Why did you show Him any affection by speaking with Him? Go! Never come near Me. Leave here at once!"

Rati Mañjarī left in a state of devastation. She fell down in a corner outside the *kuñja* in despair, and within, Rādhārānī also lamented. When Rādhārānī could no longer tolerate being separated, Lalitā-devī brought Rati back to Rādhārānī. Then Lalitā said to Śrīmatījī, "Will You forgive her and look just once in her direction?"

Dāsa Gosvāmī says, "You have patience and tolerance, please forgive me. What was my fault? Amidst a thousand things Kṛṣṇa said, I only gave a momentary reply and looked at Him for a moment from the corner of my eyes."

Those *mañjarīs* and *sakhīs* who are in Rādhārānī's group have this difficulty. Rādhārānī is not pleased if they have relation with any other.

In the first verse of *Vilāpa-kusumāñjali*, Rādhārānī gave indication for Kṛṣṇa to go to Rūpa, and Rādhārānī watched, 'What will Rūpa do?' Like if I told you, 'Do this work.' Then I will watch what you do, and if you do any error, I will correct you. What did Rūpa Mañjarī do? She ran away when Kṛṣṇa came to her. However, Rati Mañjarī spoke with Kṛṣṇa, therefore Rādhārānī became upset. If she had not spoken with Kṛṣṇa, then Rādhārānī would have been happy ten or twenty times more, and Kṛṣṇa as well.

Kṛṣṇa also would be happier if Rati had completely ignored Him, and He would have teased her even more, embracing her from behind, kissing her neck and then saying, "Won't you speak to Me?" Kṛṣṇa would fold His hands to her a thousand times if she completely ignored Him.

This mood is essential. Therefore, from an external perspective, Rūpa Gosvāmī instructed, '*vaco-vegam*' for *sādhakas*, and for those in the highest position, this is applied to a much greater extent.

Once, a policeman came and spoke with me while I was cutting vegetables in Mathurā, near the kitchen in Keśavajī Gauḍīya Maṭha. Śrīla Gurudeva was sitting in a chair on the other side of the temple courtyard. After watching me speak to the policeman for sometime, he began shouting, "Why are you talking so much? What is the need? Why do you have so much affection for this outside man?"

The policeman became astonished, got up and left. There is a very strong bond between the servant and served. If one is someone's *svapakṣa*, any slight deviation will not be tolerated, even if it is of no great significance.

tavaivāsmi tavaivāsmi na jīvāmi tvayā vinā
iti vijñāya devi tvaṁ naya māṁ caraṇāntikam

Vilāpa-kusumāñjali 96

I am Yours! I am Yours! I cannot live without You! O Devī, please understand this and bring me to Your lotus feet.

"O Rādhike, You are my heart, my soul. Everything I possess is Yours. You have complete *adhikāra* over me. I am Yours, I am Yours! Without You, I cannot stay one moment in this world. Please, please, give me shelter at Your lotus feet. I desire nothing other than the shelter of Your lotus feet."

Tavaivāsmi tavaivāsmi means, "I offer myself to You, I am Yours. I don't know anything without You. I am Yours, I am Yours, I cannot live without You." Why is this repeated? Is once not enough? The first 'I am Yours' means, "Many *mañjarīs* are close to You. May they accept me, give me shelter, and a chance to serve You. I am poor, fallen, and full of faults, but please accept me." The second 'I am Yours' means, "I am praying to Your senior authorities, the *sakhīs*. May they accept and teach me, not reject me. May they call me forward and give me a drop of their love, otherwise I am dry. How can I stay with You without any love and affection?"

If there is no love and affection, then one *brahmacārī* or devotee cannot remain following *bhakti*. He will be dry and suffering in *māyā*. If one devotee helps another, then devotion can grow in such a favorable environment. If a senior devotee nourishes junior devotees with his love and affection, the juniors' devotion will become strong, and they will gradually become senior in *bhakti*, and will bestow love and affection to others and help them grow as well. This flow will then run on continuously.

In this verse, Rati Mañjarī laments, "Aho! Devī, I have no one else in this world other than You! I am only Yours! I am only Yours! I cannot live without You for a single moment! Please bestow the shelter of Your lotus feet. I cannot go to any other, look at any other, nor have any dealing or connection with any other. I am Yours alone, Yours alone, Yours alone!"

"What is the need to promise so many times?" Śrīmatījī asks.

"If I spoke with anyone," Rati replies, "it wasn't for my own happiness. If anyone asks about You, then I feel the need to speak for Your sake. And if I don't answer, then He teases me, 'O stubborn one! O exalted arrogant maidservant of Your proud mistress. You are so exalted that you can't spare me even a moment to speak.' Then, when I said a few words, You became angered. I tell You sincerely that I am Yours, I am Yours, I am Yours! I cannot live another minute without You. Please give me shelter at Your feet. You are the reason I am living. Not seeing Your lotus feet, I cannot survive for even a moment. Please give me place at Your feet and don't make me separate from You for even a moment.

"Lalitā-devī is extremely dear to You, I am not so dear to You as she is. I made a mistake, but Lalitā-devi is very close to You. Please listen to Her request and accept me back in Your good graces. Don't keep me away from You."

Now Rati Mañjarī prays to Lalitā-devī, "Please, by any means, remove Svāminī's *māna*. If you can't do this great task, who will I go to for shelter? And only having Her speak to me again is not enough; may She grant me Her intimate service. Otherwise, if She shrugs and says, 'Okay, I forgave her, no problem,' but doesn't give me service again, keeping me at a distance, then what will be my position? Please petition Her on my behalf. If She doesn't give me Her intimate service, I will die."

Dāsa Gosvāmī was in the highest state of separation in his *sādhaka* form. Even in *mānasī-sevā*, one cannot be deviated in service and dedication to one's worshipable beloved.

Once, one thirsty man came to the cottage of Lokanātha dāsa Gosvāmī and asked for water. Receiving no answer, He next went to the *kuṭīra* of Narottama dāsa Ṭhākura and begged for water. When Narottama dāsa Ṭhākura gave water to this thirsty man, Lokanātha dāsa Gosvāmī became upset and said, "Leave this place! If you want to serve others, then there is no need to stay here. You have no desire for *bhajana*. Go and serve others." It was Kṛṣṇa who had come. There were many homes nearby in the village, why would anyone come to a Bābājī's *kuṭīra* for water? Anyone could go drink water from a well. Why would one come and beg for a glass of water from Bābājīs? But Kṛṣṇa came to test Narottama, knowing, "He is on Rādhārānī's side. Let me see what he does."

When Lokanātha dāsa Gosvāmī saw that Narottama dāsa Ṭhākura had some softness towards Kṛṣṇa, that he had become a little favorable to Kṛṣṇa, he said, "Go serve Him and His followers."

The situation is perilous for those solely dedicated to Rādhārānī. If they go a little to one side or another, then She has great *māna*. Breaking that *māna* is not easy.

sva-kuṇḍaṁ tava lolākṣi sa-priyāyāḥ sad aspadam
atraiva mama saṁvāsa ihaiva mama saṁsthitiḥ
Vilāpa-kusumāñjali 97

O restless-eyed one, Your lake is the eternal dwelling-place of You and Your beloved. Here only will I reside and here alone will I stay.

Dāsa Gosvāmī says, "Rādhā-kuṇḍa is extremely dear to You. Inside this *kuṇḍa* there is not only water, rather the mellows of all Your love are present here. All the *sakhīs*' and *mañjarīs*' love is present here as well. I stay on the bank of Your Rādhā-kuṇḍa without any qualification, but my eyes search in all directions to see from which way You are coming. The *mañjarīs* and *sakhīs* will call me and show me the pathway to Your lotus feet in a secluded grove. They will give me permission to reside here eternally."

Śrīmatī may then say, "Why are you distressed? You are already living here at Rādhā-kuṇḍa, performing *bhajana*. What problem do you have?"

"No, no, no, I have this body now. Gaurahari offered me to His near and dear Svarūpa Dāmodara, who sent me here to Rādhā-kuṇḍa. But now this body is very old. Soon it will leave me."

"Are you sad because of this?"

"No, no, no, I am not sad or afraid of leaving my body, but I want to permanently serve You in the form of a *mañjarī*. Please give this to me. Don't give me a big rich post or make me wealthy and healthy and send me far away."

Dāsa Gosvāmī prays, "May I have eternal residence here at Rādhā-kuṇḍa." What is the meaning? This means, "I will serve You while You engage in intimate pastimes with Kṛṣṇa, ready to do anything needed. I will fan You, massage Your lotus feet, and make Your bed. I will stay here for all services, not going anywhere."

Dāsa Gosvāmī next prays, "I am staying here, but I am unqualified. Yet, You are searching for me, 'Where is Rati? Where did she go?' Then I say, 'I am here, with You. Don't worry. Why are You looking at me with restless eyes? Wherever Kṛṣṇa is present, I will bring Him to Your *kuñja* by any ploy. I know how to catch Him. But if I speak with Kṛṣṇa to bring Him back, will You be angered? I will teach Him how to break Your *māna*, but for this, please don't become upset with me.

"You engage in loving pastimes with Kṛṣṇa at Rādhā-kuṇḍa. May I reside here eternally. If I am always present, I can assist Him in pleasing You. I do not want to leave this service for any other engagement."

he śrī-sarovara sadā tvayi sā mad-īśā
preṣṭhena sārdham iha khelati kāma-raṅgaiḥ
tvaṁ cet priyāt priyam atīva tayor itīmaṁ
hā darśayādya kṛpayā mama jīvitaṁ tam
Vilāpa-kusumāñjali 98

O beautiful Lake, my mistress eternally enjoys pastimes with Her beloved on your shore. If you are most dear to Them, then please mercifully show me now my mistress, who is my life and soul.

Raghunātha dāsa Gosvāmī says, "O Rādhā-kuṇḍa, my mistress, Rādhārānī, stays in a *kuñja-kuṭīra* on your bank. She gives *darśana* there and plays openly, without restriction. Kṛṣṇa also comes freely for Her *darśana*. You are very near and dear to Them. I pray to you to please grant me *darśana* of my mistress. In your beautiful waters, Kṛṣṇa dallies with Śrīmatī in varieties of love-play. Sometimes He embraces Her beneath the water of Rādhā-kuṇḍa, kissing Her neck, cheek and lips, and caressing Her bosom and other limbs."

This Rādhā-kuṇḍa is supremely dear to Rādhā-Kṛṣṇa. Why? This lake is completely filled with *rasa*. Which *rasa*?

Mādhurya-rasa. In this place that energy is present, which is the most exalted and strongest current of *mamatā*, possessive love. This current does not exist to such an extreme in any other location. By coming to Rādhā-kuṇḍa, a powerful urge and enthusiasm comes from the flow of *mādhurya* there, and desire comes to express one's love. In other places, one may become tired, apathetic, or remain distant. But here there is no separation; there is complete closeness.

kṣaṇam api tava saṅgaṁ na tyajed eva devi
tvam asi samavayastvān narma-bhūmir yad asyāḥ
iti sumukhi viśākhe darśayitvā mad-īśāṁ
mama viraha-hatāyāḥ prāṇa-rakṣāṁ kuruṣva
Vilāpa-kusumāñjali 99

O fair-faced Viśākhe, My mistress will not leave your company for even a moment. Because You are both the same age, you are the realm of Her playful joking pastimes. Please save my life from the affliction of separation and show me my Svāminī.

Dāsa Gosvāmī prays, "O Viśākhe, you are my *guru*. You teach how to serve my Svāminī, Rādhikā. You never leave Her even for a moment. I pray to you, please bring me to my Svāminī. You are of the same age as my Svāminī, and similar in nature to Her. I don't want to leave your association. You bestow *darśana* of my mistress. I am weeping in separation. Please save my life."

Why does he pray like this? Śrīmatī Rādhārāṇī doesn't like to give up Viśākhā's company for a moment. Śrīmatī always keeps Viśākhā near. They are very close friends. When Kṛṣṇa comes forcefully to kiss Śrīmatī, She sometimes places Viśākhā before Him. Kṛṣṇa then jokes and plays with Viśākhā, but Viśākhā moves aside and pushes Him towards Rādhikā. Why? Rādhikā's followers do not desire to independently meet with Kṛṣṇa. When Viśākhā sends Kṛṣṇa to Rādhārāṇī, she doesn't leave the *kuñja*.

Why? So that Kṛṣṇa doesn't harass Her too much. When He tries to, Viśākhā reprimands Him, "Move! No more." Kṛṣṇa is not satisfied. He has desire to meet with Rādhikā, but Viśākhā takes Him away to increase His eagerness even more.

She says, "Why are You so hard with my Kiśorī? Her skin is scratched from Your attacks!" Viśākhā takes Rādhārānī into a private quarter and applies a cooling sandal paste on Her limbs, while saying, "I shouldn't have allowed Kṛṣṇa to come. Now He has bruised and scratched You." Rādhārānī also desired to meet more with Kṛṣṇa, but Viśākhā took Her away to increase Her eagerness even more. Then Kṛṣṇa crept up from behind and suddenly kissed Śrīmatī, causing Her beautiful face to flush red.

"This is not appropriate!" Viśākhā exclaimed, "how many times have I told You to restrain Yourself!"

Just then, Lalitā comes in with the *mañjarīs* and says, "Send Kṛṣṇa out and bar the door of the *kuñja*."

Kṛṣṇa is sent forcibly out of the *kuñja*. Within, Lalitā and Viśākhā begin to serve and decorate Śrīmatī. Kṛṣṇa searches for a pathway in, or a gap to peek inside. By these playful actions of the *sakhīs*, His happiness is increased and *mādhurya-rasa* swells.

Dāsa Gosvāmī prays, "O worshipable Viśākhā, Rādhārānī doesn't like to leave you for even a moment. You are always joyful in Her company. Please bestow *darśana* of my mistress, saving my life. By your indication, I will also enter in the *kuñja* and apply sandal on the cut marks on Rādhārānī's cheek and chest. By your mercy, I will go and intimately serve Svāminī."

Kṛṣṇa comes and pleads to Rati Mañjarī at the *kuñja* entrance, "Please let me enter the *kuñja*. I will not disturb Śrīmatī any more. I will only go and sit a short distance from Her, and won't tease or taunt Her. I swear that I won't touch Her." But He cannot live without Śrīmatī. He prays to Rati, "My life is departing in separation from Her, only you can save My life."

He tries to convince Rati Mañjarī by stroking her cheek, but Rati neglects Him and moves away, knowing Rādhārānī would become angry with her if she allowed Kṛṣṇa to affectionately caress her. Kṛṣṇa's separation from Rādhārānī is so intense, it is impossible for Him to tolerate.

hā nātha gokula-sudhākara su-prasanna-
vaktrāravinda madhura-smita he kṛpārdra
yatra tvayā viharate praṇayaiḥ priyārāt
tatraiva mām api naya priya-sevanāya
Vilāpa-kusumāñjali 100

O Lord, O nectar moon of Gokula, O You whose cheerful lotus face smiles sweetly, O You who melts with compassion! Wherever You go to enjoy loving pastimes with Your beloved, please take me there so that I can affectionately serve You.

Kṛṣṇa, who is Gokulacandra, the moon of Gokula, nourishes Gokula Mahāvana, the realm of the *gopas, gopīs,* and cows. He is always very pleased and smiling. Why? His heart is Rādhārānī's dwelling place; She is His nearest and dearest.

Kṛṣṇa is sweet and smiling, with a very soft heart. If anyone comes to Him, He desires to send them to the Vraja-devīs. This is His deep desire. Kṛṣṇa never keeps one nearby Himself. He looks, "Who has come to Me? What is their desire?" Observing their desires, he sends some to Mathurā, some to Dvārakā, some to Earth, and some to heavenly planets. However, if anyone has a little bit of respect and faith for the Vraja *gopīs,* Kṛṣṇa will certainly send him to Vraja-dhāma. He will bestow deep affection and love so as to nourish one's service. This affection is not small; it is unlimited and continuously flowing.

Dāsa Gosvāmī prays, "O Gokulacandra, You distribute nectar to the hearts of everyone. When You are pleased, You make everyone pleased. O merciful one, Rādhārāṇī is very dear to You. Please send me to Her, and there I will learn the process of love.

"O Gokula-sudhākara, the embodiment of nectar, when You speak, a shower of nectar drenches me. When I see You, it is as if nectar is raining upon me. Please take me to that place where You engage in loving pastimes with Śrīmatī Rādhikā. As You dally with Śrīmatījī, I will be close at hand to serve You when You become weary, giving a glass of cool juice, water, or a honey-drink.

"O beautiful one, when You glance at any living beings with Your lotus eyes, You acquire their hearts and cause them to fall madly in love with You. Dallying in the hearts of Your beloveds, external meeting is not required to feel the bliss of union. Merely seeing You with Śrīmatī, my heart overflows with joy."

Hearing this prayer, Kṛṣṇa smiles and says, "This is not a request generally heard of. Still, I grant your wish. Not all people receive this qualification. But you are very dear to Rādhikā. Knowing this, I fulfill your prayer."

lakṣmīr yad-aṅghri-kamalasya nakhāñcalasya
saundarya-bindum api nārhati labdhum īśe
sā tvaṁ vidhāsyasi na cen mama netra-dānaṁ
kīm jīvitena mama duḥkha-davāgnidena

Vilāpa-kusumāñjali 101

O my Goddess, Your beauty is such that Lakṣmī, the Goddess of Fortune Herself, is unable to attain even a drop of the beauty of the tips of Your lotus toenails. If You do not give Your *darṣana* in charity to my eyes, then what is the use of my life, ablaze with a great forest fire of sufferings?

Lakṣmī-devī always serves Lord Nārāyaṇa, massaging His feet and sometimes placing them on her chest or head. She is so dear to Lord Nārāyaṇa that He keeps her in the form of a golden line on His chest. Yet, she doesn't have the ability to enter Vraja and witness the pastimes of Kṛṣṇa with Śrīmatī Rādhārāṇī.

Knowing this benediction is not even granted to the goddess of fortune Lakṣmī-devī, Dāsa Gosvāmī prays, "Please grant me Your favor, allowing me to serve in Your intimate pastimes. If You bestow transcendental vision, I will be able to see Your pastimes, and my tendency to serve will increase. If You don't show me mercy, there is no value to my life and I shall give it up at once. Give me the fortune of witnessing Your pastimes."

What is the meaning of *darśana*? Is merely witnessing pastimes enough? Dāsa Gosvāmī prays, "I will favorably serve in Your pastimes."

One thing is ordinary, or external, *darśana*, but a higher *darśana* is that which is infused with transcendental vision and knowledge.

Dāsa Gosvāmī entreats Śrīmatī, "If You do not bestow the gift of transcendental vision to me, then I will be consumed in this forest fire of misery that is burning me."

What is this fire of suffering? "I am not dear to You." How is this? "If You do not bestow qualification to serve in Your pastimes, having not attained my aspiration, I will soon give up my life."

In this world, Lakṣmī's influence is all-pervasive; she commands everyone's respect and everyone desires to attain her. Everyone hankers after respect, health, and wealth. Lakṣmī-devī distributes these things. Then, going near these things, the *jīvas* become blind. Why is this? Does Lakṣmī not give light to their eyes? By collecting mundane things from Lakṣmī and staying near them, the eyes are fixed there and cannot see anything else. Then how can one transcend this world and *māyā*, and come to Śrīmatī Rādhārāṇī in Vṛndāvana-dhāma? This is not possible.

Many times, Śrīla Gurudeva told the story of a wife and husband who were devotees of Viṣṇu, named Raka and Baka. Daily, they went to the forest and collected dry wood, that they brought and sold in the market to maintain themselves. Seeing their condition, Nārada Ṛṣi became disturbed and said to Lord Nārāyaṇa, "Your devotees are working very hard, tolerating all conditions. They are very poor. Why don't You send Lakṣmī to help them?"

"They do not like Lakṣmī," the Lord replied. "If I send her, they will not accept her."

"No, please send her, my Lord."

Lord Nārāyaṇa gave him some gold and jewels and said, "Take these to those devotees."

"Okay, I am going," Nārada Ṛṣi said.

"I am coming as well," Lord Nārāyaṇa said.

Nārada Ṛṣi came with Lord Nārāyaṇa, and went to the forest where Raka and Baka were on their way to collect wood. Nārada Ṛṣi placed the gold and jewels on the pathway and hid behind a tree to watch what they would do. The husband was in front and the wife was behind him. As the husband came forward, he saw that many gold coins and jewels were on the path. He used the sand on the pathway to quickly cover the coins before his wife came. But when she caught up with him, she said, "What are you doing? Why are you wasting your time covering dirt with other dirt?"

"I thought you would be attracted to this gold and want to take it home."

"Why would I waste time with this? I am very happy as we are. Let's go."

Then Raka and Baka continued on their way, without looking back at the gold or even once thinking to take it.

Lord Nārāyaṇa then said to Nārada, "Just see, My devotees have no desire for wealth. They don't want to divide their heart at all from Me."

Lakṣmī comes and tries to serve the Vrajavāsīs, but they do not accept what she offers. By accepting opulence, the heart will be divided from Vraja.

Therefore Dāsa Gosvāmī prays, "Please, give me eyes so that I will watch only You, Your *mañjarīs* and *sakhīs*, not Lakṣmī, or any other group. Otherwise, if I think of Lakṣmī, she will come and try to cheat and bribe me into her company. This would be like jumping into a forest fire of suffering."

nityārtidena vittena durlabhenātma-mṛtyunā
gṛhāpatyāpta-paśubhiḥ kā prītiḥ sādhitaiś calaiḥ
Śrīmad-Bhāgavatam 11.3.19

Wealth is a perpetual source of distress, it is most difficult to acquire, and it is virtual death for the soul. What satisfaction does one actually gain from his wealth? Similarly, how can one gain ultimate or permanent happiness from one's so-called home, children, relatives, and domestic animals, which are all maintained by one's hard-earned money?

One who accepts opulence suffers in his present life, when he leaves his present body, and in lives to come.

āśā-bharair amṛta-sindhu-mayaiḥ kathañcit
kālo mayāti-gamitaḥ kila sāmpratarṁ hi
tvaṁ cet kṛpāṁ mayi vidhāsyasi naiva kiṁ me
prāṇair vrajena ca varoru bakāriṇāpi
Vilāpa-kusumāñjali 102

O beautiful-thighed one, I have spent all my time here, aspiring after oceans of nectar. Now, if You are not kind to me, then what is the use of my life, my living in Vraja and even Kṛṣṇa, the enemy of Baka?

Dāsa Gosvāmī prays, "O Rādhike, my hope is that You will give me one drop from the ocean of Your compassion. If You do not give me any mercy, I do not want to reside in Rādhā-kuṇḍa, have any connection with Kṛṣṇa, Vraja, or anything else.

"Kṛṣṇa is the ocean of nectar. Drowning in the ocean of His beauty, all beings become maddened. But You control Him and keep Him near You at all times. With the wish to attain Your service, I pass my life in great distress. If You don't bestow mercy upon me, I will give up my life.

"I have only one aspiration. If any hypocrisy or ulterior desire is lurking within me, and because of that You are not accepting me, please slay such a desire or nature. Please don't deprive me of Your mercy! Remove all obstacles and bring me to Your lotus feet. At every moment, in every circumstance, enable me to remain close to You. This is my hope. I maintain my life simply by this hope. I want nothing else but to one-pointedly serve You and Your beloved in a secluded grove. If You were to say, 'Would You not feel any shyness or shame?' I reply, 'I am not against You or separate from You; I am Your's alone.' If You were to say, 'If someone else is present, some obstacle would come in My meetings with Kṛṣṇa,' I reply, 'I am not separate from You. Thus I cannot become an obstacle in Your meetings.' "

What is the mood of the *mañjarīs*? Śrīla Bhaktivinoda Ṭhākura demonstrates this in his prayer:

> *śrī kṛṣṇa-virahe, rādhikāra daśā, āmi to' sahite nāri*
> *yugala-milana, sukhera kāraṇa, jīvana chāḍite pāri*

> I am absolutely unable to tolerate Śrī Rādhikā's pitiable condition when She is suffering in separation from Śrī Kṛṣṇa, but I am fully prepared to immediately give up my life for the sake of Their happy reunion.

Dāsa Gosvāmī prays, "There is no question of disturbance from my service, either to me or You. And even if there may be, please cleanse me and accept me as Your own, keeping me near You always. I am only a small *mañjarī*; I am not skilled and my body is not strong. Please bless me, that I become beautiful and expert in all manners of service, so that I may be able to please You and Your beloved.

tvaṁ cet kṛpāmayi kṛpāṁ mayi duḥkhitāyāṁ
naivātanor atitarāṁ kim iha pralāpaiḥ
tvat-kuṇḍa-madhyam api tad-bahu-kālam eva
saṁsevyamānam api kiṁ nu kariṣyatīha
Vilāpa-kusumāñjali 103

O merciful one, if You will not give Your great mercy to this suffering one, then what was the use of all these lamentations and all my long service to Your lake?

Dāsa Gosvāmī prays, "If You don't give me Your blessings, then, bitterly weeping, I will beseech You, 'I have waited for so long to serve You. If You don't give any mercy, I will soon give up my life. I am very sad. See how I am suffering and praying everyday. Do not wait. Please come and accept me, and give me the chance to serve You at Rādhā-kuṇḍa. I will continuously serve here.'

ayi praṇaya-śālini praṇaya-puṣṭa-dāsyāptaye
prakāmam api rodanaiḥ pracura-duḥkha-dagdhātmanā
vilāpa-kusumāñjalir hṛdi nidhāya pādāmbuje
mayā bata samarpitas tava tanotu tuṣṭiṁ manāk
Vilāpa-kusumāñjali 104

O affectionate one, loudly weeping and yearning for Your loveful service, I clasp Your lotus feet to my burning heart and place these laments at Your lotus feet as a bouquet of flowers. May they give You a little pleasure.

Dāsa Gosvāmī prays, "O Rādhike, I will be Your servant. I yearn for Your servitorship. I am crying to You and offering this *Vilāpa-kusumāñjali* at Your lotus feet. Please be satisfied with me and bestow Your intimate service. May Your lotus feet always be present in my heart. This is my prayer. If You don't accept me, I will burn in the fire of Your separation. I request You to please, please accept me.

"I have lamented to You in so many ways. If anyone loves You and wants to serve You, Your heart is too soft to reject that person; You accept that soul as Your own. If the soul is unqualified, then You send her to the company of Rūpa Mañjarī for training. Rūpa Mañjarī then gradually teaches her the perfect manners of service, and once she is favorably taught, Rūpa then brings her to You and gives her a chance for service. Please nourish me with Your love and help me attain the highest state of perfection—service of Your lotus feet. I am being consumed in the fire of sorrow. Therefore, I am weeping to You, offering my heart to You and praying again and again. Please accept my woeful entreaties at Your lotus feet. This is my offering of love to You. I am calling out to You for mercy. I am crying out and inviting You to come accept me and bring me into Your service in transcendental Vraja. My mind is not able to seek any other thing. I will not be swayed by the invitation of Kṛṣṇa or by the bribe of any group opposing You. I am Yours, only Yours."

Śrīla Gurudeva's Upadeśāvalī

Essential Instructions of Paramārādhyatama Bhaktabāndhav
Śrī Śrīmad Bhaktivedānta Nārāyaṇa Gosvāmī Mahārāja

1) Those who do not worship Bhagavān, who is the father of the universe and maintainer of everyone, are ignorant fools and killers of their very selves.

2) *Bhagavad-bhakti* is the subject matter expounded in the Vedas, Upaniṣads, Smṛtis, and Purāṇas.

3) The constitutional nature of the living beings is service to Bhagavān. Because of a particular circumstance, living beings have forgotten to serve Bhagavān and, since time immemorial, have fallen into the cycle of birth and death, where they burn in the three-fold miseries of material existence. By the mercy of Bhagavān or the *bhaktas*, the living beings can follow the path of *bhagavad-bhakti*, and then become situated in their original constitional nature, where they will taste the blissful *rasa* of serving Bhagavān.

4) *Harināma-saṅkīrtana* is the highest *sādhana* and *sādhya* of the living beings.

5)

harer nāma harer nāma harer nāmaiva kevalam
kalau nāsty eva nāsty eva nāsty eva gatir anyathā

In this age of quarrel and hypocrisy, the only means of deliverance is chanting the holy name, chanting the holy name, chanting the holy name of the Lord. There is no other way. There is no other way. There is no other way.

6) Vrajendra-nandana Śrī Kṛṣṇa is the ultimate manifestation of Godhead. He is the ocean of all nectarean mellows and the possessor of all potencies.

7) Vrajendra-nandana Śrī Kṛṣṇa is beyond Māyā; He is the reservoir of all transcendental qualities; He is an ocean of unconditional, causeless mercy, and He is *bhakta-vatsala*, affectionate to His devotees.

8) Transcendental to Māyā, the intrinsic transcendental form of Vrajendra-nandana Śrī Kṛṣṇa is the youthful dancer who wears the attire of a cowherd boy and who is holding the flute.

9) Firm faith in Śrī Gurudeva is the backbone of *bhajana*. Without serving *sad-guru* and receiving his mercy, one can never enter the realm of *bhakti*.

10) The bona fide spiritual master is expert and realized in Vedic literature; he possesses complete realization of Bhagavān; he is detached from material sense objects; and he is the crest-jewel of devotees who is always absorbed in chanting the names of Bhagavān. By accepting the shelter of such a *sad-guru* it is possible to enter the practice of *śuddha-bhakti*, pure devotional service, otherwise not.

11) To endeavor to please the minds of sense enjoyers; to accumulate material objects and to remain engrossed in sense enjoyment; to foster desire for the attainment of heaven or liberation—these are not the characteristics of a genuine spiritual master. One should remain far distant from such imposters (who are engaged in the above activities while posing as *gurus*.)

12) *Kṛṣṇa-prema* is the one and only ultimate goal for all living beings.

13) The *Śrīmad-Bhāgavatam* is the spotless evidence for all mankind.

14) The Vraja-gopīs' worship of Kṛṣṇa is the topmost form of worship.

15) Worship of God is only possible in the human form of life. Other species live for the sole purpose of enjoyment. For those in the human form of life, it is auspicious to worship Bhagavān from childhood.

16) The one and only *dharma* in Kali-yuga is the congregational chanting of Bhagavān's holy names. By the performance of *saṅkīrtana*, living beings can easily attain auspiciousness. Giving up *saṅkīrtana*, those who instruct others and who are personally inclined to perform sacrifices, austerities, *yoga*, and cultivate *jñāna* (the conception that I will merge within Brahman)—all these peoples' activities are futile. This is the proclamation of scripture.

17) If you desire your own welfare, never criticize the bhaktas. By criticizing Vaiṣṇavas, your destruction is inevitable.

18) The root cause of *bhakti* is to hear *hari-kathā* while in *sat-saṅga*. Without *sat-saṅga* the living beings can never achieve auspiciousness.

he bhupeśa he nareśa
he vraja-jana-hita-kari
he lokeśa he vareśa
he bhagavān murārī

O Lord of the Earth and all living entities, You always look after the welfare of the Vrajavāsīs. O Bhagavān Murārī, You destroy the greatest demon in Vraja—our separation from You. You are the Lord of the universe and the greatest giver of boons.

he nitāī he nimāī
he patita-uddhāraṇa-kari
he sītānātha he prāṇanātha
he tribhuvana-arthī-hari

O Nitāī, O Nimāī, You uplift the fallen souls! O Sītānātha, O Prāṇanātha, by leaving the lotus feet of Bhagavān, one experiences all forms of sufferings, but You bring the living entities back to His shelter and give eternal residence in Vraja, You thus steal away all miseries. Please bless us to achieve the mercy and service of Śrīmatī Rādhārānī.

Śrī Kṛṣṇa Caitanya Prabhu Nityānanda
Śrī Advaita Gadādhara Śrīvāsadi Gaura-bhakta-vṛnda

Hare Kṛṣṇa Hare Kṛṣṇa Kṛṣṇa Kṛṣṇa Hare Hare
Hare Rāma Hare Rāma Rāma Rāma Hare Hare

vairāgya-yug bhakti-rasaṁ prayatnair
apāyayan mām anabhīpsum andham
kṛpāmbudhir yaḥ para-duḥkha-duḥkhī
sanātanaṁ taṁ prabhum āśrayāmi

I surrender to the lotus feet of my master, Śrī Sanātana Gosvāmī, who is the bestower of *sambandha-jñāna*. He is an ocean of mercy and his heart always becomes distressed upon seeing the suffering of others. Although due to the darkness of ignorance I had no desire to taste *bhakti-rasa* imbued with renunciation, he forced me to taste it and thereby gave me knowledge of my relationship with Kṛṣṇa.

ādadānas tṛṇaṁ dantair
idaṁ yāce punaḥ punaḥ
śrīmad rūpa-padāmbhoja
dhūliḥ syāṁ janma-janmani

Taking a straw between my teeth, I beg again and again, "Oh, I want to become the dust of the lotus feet of Śrīla Rūpa Gosvāmīpāda so that I may serve him birth after birth."